Endorsements & Praise

"Thank you [Ted] for allowing me to attend your class on *Robert's Rules of Order*. Your scholarship came in handy since I am a full-time intern. Attending your class empowered me to create effective meetings immediately. I was able to use Robert's Rules on a current project that was spiraling out of control. The information you gave allowed me to conduct a meeting in a timely manner and provided an ideal framework to ensure that the project is carried out successfully. I am looking forward to revisiting my class handouts and investigating more information to help facilitate future meetings.

Thank you for providing a model in the class that was easy to follow and memorable. I am looking forward to your upcoming book.

Warmly, Juliette Broussard

Dear Ted,

I am so glad that my predecessor, the former director of the Brooklyn Free School, Allen Berger and our school played a role in inspiring *Robert's Rules for Kids*!

The Brooklyn Free School is run democratically and we know first-hand how helpful Robert's Rules can be for group process. Your book breaks these tools down so that all students, in all settings, can participate in decision-making.

You have given classrooms a great document that will improve overall learning and engagement, and assist students to become effective leaders and participants in democratic institutions for the rest of their lives.

Thank you from the bottom of our hearts for participating in this movement to democratize education!

All the best, Lily Mercogliano
Executive Director, Brooklyn Free School
"Where Children are Free to Be Themselves"

Robert's Rules for Kids and Big Kids:
A Guide to Teaching Children of All Ages the Basics of Parliamentary Procedure
2nd Edition

Wise Wit Publishing Company
Houston, Texas

Robert's Rules for Kids and Big Kids:
A Guide to Teaching Children of All Ages the Basics of Parliamentary Procedure
2nd Edition

Martha J. Haun, Ph.D., PRP

Ted Weisgal

Wise Wit Publishing Company

Houston, Texas

Robert's Rules for Kids and Big Kids:
A Guide to Teaching Children of All Ages the Basics of Parliamentary Procedure

2nd Edition

Copyright © 2017 by Martha Haun and Ted Weisgal

If you would like to share this book with another person, please purchase an additional copy for each recipient. If you're reading this book and did not purchase it, or it was not purchased for your exclusive use, please go to your favorite e-book retailer or bookstore to purchase your own copy. Thank you for respecting the hard work of the authors.

DISCLAIMER: All rights reserved. No part of this book may be used or reproduced by any means, graphic, electronic, or mechanical, including photocopying, recording, taping or by any information storage retrieval system without the written permission of the authors except in case of brief quotations embodied in critical articles or reviews, where the source is properly acknowledged. Photocopies of sample documents may be made for classroom use with appropriate copyright information.

Books may be ordered through booksellers, on-line from the printer (CreateSpace.com) and retailers, like Amazon.com, or by contacting the publisher:

> Wise Wit Publishing Company
> 12137 Stone West Drive
> Houston, Texas 77035
> www.wisewitpubco.com

The views expressed in this work are solely those of the authors and do not necessarily reflect the views of the publisher, and the publisher hereby disclaims any responsibility for them.

ISBN-13: 978-1973917595

Electronic versions are also available.

Printed in the United States of America

Contents

Preface to the 2nd Edition.. iii
Chapter 1: Introduction..1
   Preserving and Enriching the Democratic Process............................ 3
   Spiral of Silence 5
   The Application of *Robert's Rules of Order Newly Revised*
   to Habits of Mind.. 6
   The Flexibility of Robert's, Carl Sagan, and Critical Thinking 9
   Long-range Goals 11

Chapter 2: Early Elementary 13
   Teaching Kindergartners... 13
      An All-School Approach 14
      Reading Rockets – Early Elementary: K-1 17
      Dictation.. 17
      Examples.. 18
      Differentiated Instruction.. 19
   Teaching 1st Graders 20
      Scenario 20
      Alternative 1st Grade Approach 22
      Procedures in Small Boards and Committees 23-24

Chapter 3: Middle & Late Elementary 25
   Teaching 2nd and 3rd Graders 26
   Specific Outcomes: Grades 4-5 26
      Language Arts 27
      Arts, Math, Spelling, Language, Mathematics,
      Communication, Social Studies 27-28
      Cognitive, Emotional, or Behavioral Responses 28
   Activities for Late Elementary – Grades 4-5 29
      Bloom's Cognitive Levels 31
      Skills Model.. 32
      Common Stages in Group Process 33
      Math Exercise 35
      Simple Bylaws 36

Chapter 4: Middle and High School 38
   Philosophy 38
   High Expectations 39
   Bylaws 39
   Sample Minutes (simple) 40
   Committee Reports 41
   Disciplinary Procedures 41

Chapter 5: Nuts and Bolts **46**
    Voting 46
    Governing Documents 47
    Ranking Parliamentary Motions 48
    Privileged Motions 48
    Subsidiary Motions 50
    Main Motion 51
    Incidental Motions 53
    Bring Back Motions/Restoratory Motions 56
    Rules of Debate 58
    Charts of Parliamentary Motions 59-62
    Glossary of Parliamentary Terms 63

Chapter 6: History of H. M. Robert **69**

Chapter 7: Scripting: Sample Script **73**
    Using Scripts 73
    Script: Parliamentary Drill on the Precedence of Motions 73-83

Chapter 8: Meet the Authors **85**
    Martha's Story 85
    Martha's Acknowledgments 90
    Ted's Story 91
    Ted's Acknowledgments 97

REFERENCES **99**

APPENDICES **102**
    Appendix A. Bylaws of the Student Council of Furr High School,
      Houston, Texas 103
    Appendix B. Bylaws of the Jack Yates High School Student
    Government, Houston, Texas 110
    Appendix C. Event Guidelines 118
    Appendix D. Sample Agenda 121
    Appendix E. Sample Annual Calendar 122
    Appendix F. Sports Column, Los Angeles Herald-Examiner, 1962 123
    Appendix G. Chart of Motions 125-128

PREFACE

"The Whole is Greater Than the Sum of Its Parts."
—Aristotle (384-322BC)

When we ask adults if they are familiar with *Robert's Rules of Order Newly Revised (RONR)*, about 80% say "no." If you're one of them, you're in good company. We cite several scholars in Chapter 1 for whom we have great respect: Drs. Robert Putnam, Daniel Goleman, and Tony Wagner, all of Harvard; Dr. Jeffrey Pfeffer, Stanford; Dr. Carl Sagan, Cornell; Dr. Elisabeth Noelle-Neumann, University of Chicago; and educational philosopher Sir Ken Robinson; as well as nationally syndicated columnist Ruben Navarrette, Jr. They all appear to be unaware of the value of *Robert's Rules*. When it would have been appropriate to mention *Robert's* in their works, they didn't. Those who are familiar with *Robert's* usually add that they don't like it. When we ask individually and in groups, "Have you ever had what we are proposing—formal training in *Robert's Rules*?" almost everyone says "no."

RONR is a document that's referenced in the bylaws of almost every non-profit organization with which we've been associated over the last 50 years, hundreds. Nevertheless, there are only a few people advocating that it be taught. Two nearly long-forgotten speeches are referenced in Chapter 1. The speakers made a strong case for teaching *RONR* in school but, so far, their pleadings have been ignored.

For us, this has been an amazing journey. We hope it is for you as well.

This book is designed for teachers and their students from kindergarten to the 12th grade. Classroom teachers are our primary audience, but we hope what we've written appeals to everyone interested in the positive results that come from learning the key elements of this collaborative, democratic decision-making tool.

This is the third book on this subject. The first was *Robert's Rules for Kids...A Guide to Teaching Children from K-5 the Basics of Parliamentary Procedure*. After it came out, we learned what should have been obvious: some students are not going to get this material until middle or high school. So, urged on by a high school principal, we embarked on writing a book for all students in all grades. That book has the same title as this one but we've learned some important things along the way. Taking a page from *Robert's Rules of Order Newly Revised (RONR)* which is now in its 11th edition, we're sharing in this second edition of *Robert's Rules for Kids & Big Kids...A Guide to Teaching Children of All Ages the Basics of Parliamentary Procedure* what we've learned. An important addition is the quotation, above, from Aristotle. In 10 words, this ancient genius captures the value of the group process, synergy, in contrast to people working autonomously. To illustrate this point, hold out an open hand. Any finger, by itself, is weak compared to a fist.

In the Introduction to *RONR*, the authors state that "the holding of assemblies of elders...is doubtless a custom older than history." While there are achievements that appear to be accomplished by individuals, if you analyze virtually any of them, you'll discover, as did Aristotle, the benefits of the group process.

Public education in the United States is a 13-year process. Coincidentally, it took the same amount of time, 13 years, for Henry Martyn Robert to go from chairing a disastrous meeting in New Bedford, Massachusetts, during the Civil War to writing the forerunner to *Robert's Rules of Order* which he titled *Pocket Manual of Rules of Order for Deliberative Assemblies*. We believe that by developing a working knowledge of *Robert's Rules* throughout these 13 school years, students will become comfortable in meetings and many will become active participants and proficient leaders for the rest of their lives. We think society needs to do a better job of engaging people and encouraging them to weigh in on decisions that affect their lives. We believe this book contributes significantly to that end.

If school began when children were four years old, we'd recommend starting this process then. We've surprised experienced educators by showing them that these preschoolers are as excited as older students when given the opportunity to participate in age-appropriate aspects of this activity. Through study and practice we hope entire student bodies learn this skill. We provide a variety of concrete examples on how to do it but invite you to modify them to meet your circumstances. One option, fleshed out in Chapter 2, is for students in 4th and 5th grades to team up with kids in the lower grades to learn one of the easiest components of *Robert's*, the seven rules for committees and small boards. While they're doing this, they'll advance their reading skills using a tool, dictation, from the award-winning PBS television show, *Reading Rockets*. In the 2nd and 3rd grades (Chapter 3), we propose spending time teaching the vocabulary of Robert's and how he has it *ordered*. In the 4th and 5th grades (also in Chapter 3) we add elections and leadership opportunities through a Student Council that involves every student in the school. In higher grades, as students hone skills, their vocabulary can become more sophisticated and their use of motions more masterful.

In the motion picture, "Sound of Music," Julie Andrews sings *Do-Re-Me*:
> "Let's start at the very beginning. A very good place to start. When you read, you begin with A-B-C. When you sing you begin with do-re-mi."

That would be ideal in terms of learning *Robert's*. It would be great if every child started learning it in kindergarten but students can't be asked to start school all over again.

For students in middle and high school, we urge teachers to adapt what we've created. All the information is vital but older kids can learn it more quickly. In Chapter 4 there is a nine-step guide to help write perhaps the most vital document an organization can have, bylaws. Through the practical application of this information, teachers can create an excellent starting point for establishing a student government regardless of the age group. Students need to learn these basics. The best way might be by concurrently reviewing committee rules and the vocabulary of *Robert's*, and then by adding student council responsibilities. *Robert's* is an outstanding tool because it can be modified via Standing and Special Rules to meet the needs of all students.

Understanding what these six sentences mean is vital:

- I move that…
- I second it.
- Will the maker of the motion please speak in favor of the motion?
- Is there a speaker against the motion?
- All those in favor say aye.
- All those opposed say no.

We delve into this in "Chapter 5: Nuts and Bolts." These six sentences are used in the United States Congress and the British Parliament. But don't let students get confused. While there is a great deal in common and Robert used both of those bodies as resources for his document, there are significant differences. For example, *RONR* does not allow filibustering and speakers may not yield their time. When students have a solid understanding of *Robert's*, they will be more prepared to understand what's going on when they watch Congress or the Parliament. Familiarity with this subject may even get them thinking about running for political office. They will be more prepared than someone who has never studied this subject. But having knowledge of *Robert's* can be confusing if they don't understand that there are differences between the rules of Congress, Parliament, and *RONR*.

Until now, no one has written a book designed to promote synergistic thinking in grades K-12. In sports, coaches constantly promote teamwork and the virtues of practice. In the classroom, teamwork is the exception. The practice of it is certainly not the rule. The U.S. and other countries have been able to send people to outer space; men have walked on the moon. On earth, though, we've yet to master the art of resolving our differences through dialogue. There's no denying that schools are not always idyllic. Sometimes both dialogue and other forms of behavior can be painful. Both *RONR* and our book address that. One of the schools that inspired this book, Furr High School, Houston, has a student court. We've got evidence that it can be among the most effective ways to administer justice and improve future behavior in a school. Details about Disciplinary Procedures appear in Chapter 4.

Perhaps it's too audacious to suggest that this book will move us forward toward a world where everyone can live in peace but that is our hope. With this training, we believe people can interact civilly and play a part in the process.

The authors wish to acknowledge their indebtedness to Henry M. Robert III, Daniel H. Honemann, Thomas J. Balch, Daniel E. Seabold, and Shmuel Gerber for their work on the Eleventh Edition of Robert's Rules of Order Newly Revised (RONR). It is upon that book that this guide is based.

CHAPTER 1: INTRODUCTION

When we were completing this book—a book we view as largely positive—we faced a dilemma. We didn't want to give undue attention to *Roberta's Rules of Order* by Alice Collier Cochran[1.1] But then we came across one review of her book. It said: "Skip this dangerous book. … I strongly recommend against purchasing this book unless you are in an organization which has already (foolishly) adopted it as their parliamentary authority...."

Robert's Rules of Order,[1.2] not *Roberta's Rules of Order*, is the universal standard for democratic decision-making. There are over five and one-half million copies in print. We hope you will develop, as we have, an appreciation for its value and history dating back to 1876.

Roberta's Rules of Order, written by Alice Cochran in 2004, is obviously a "Johnnie-come-lately." On the cover of her book, Ms. Cochran asks the question, "Who is Robert and why do we still follow his rules anyway?" In response, we rhetorically ask, who is Roberta and why should we follow her? Roberta, we know, is a fictitious name and a clever title for a book, but when it bases its existence on half-truths, then it becomes suspect.

Cochran writes, "*Robert's Rules of Order* states that smaller boards… can write or modify 'Special Rules' that can be used instead of or in combination with parliamentary rules." She goes on to say, "My book…will help you create these Special Rules for your organization." She asserts that her methods are "more flexible…."

On pages 23 and 24, we share with you from *Robert's Rules of Order Newly Revised (RONR 11th ed.)* seven simple rules for small boards and committees. Ms. Cochran did not do this; it's antithetical to the premise of her book. There are other books that steer people completely astray. Recently we went to a Barnes & Noble bookstore and surveyed every book (about 30) in their section on leadership. Not one referred to Robert's Rules. It appears that the scholars who have written these books are oblivious to RONR.

Dr. Robert Putnam, author of the bestseller *Bowling Alone: The Collapse and Revival of American Community*[1.3] wrote that organizations are smaller and less significant than they once were. Putnam's book focuses on social isolation and how it is impacting our society. He writes that fewer people join organizations and teams, like bowling leagues, than in the past and so are now "bowling alone." He says this disconnects us all but, like every writer on this problem today, he overlooks what we suggest is a fundamental solution.

Stanford Graduate School of Business professor Jeffrey Pfeffer recognized the leadership-*followership* problem in his 2015 book, *Leadership BS: Fixing Workplaces and Careers One Truth at a Time.*[1.4] He writes, "Corporate training in the U.S. is a $70 billion market, and 35% of that is spent on management and leadership training." But, he notes, "none of that is working...the workplace today is as dysfunctional as ever."

We agree with him that there is need for better leaders. He may not know it but RONR is a key tool to becoming one.

In some cases, we think that there is an effort to dilute RONR, the gold standard for both leadership skills and democratic decision-making. Maybe it is ignorance but we think some people find it in their interest to keep society ignorant.

In the early days of the development of electricity, Thomas Edison had a battle with George Westinghouse over whether the United States' standard for electricity would be alternating current (AC) or direct current (DC). Imagine the chaos had this dispute gone unresolved. Because of technical and cost efficiency reasons, AC won. Only in 2016 are scientists finding ways to use A/C and D/C in combination. We think a similar thing is true for RONR. In group social interaction, there is dysfunction because there is no standard. We believe RONR is the standard that should be taught. Of course, right now, there are a plethora of authors, books, and ideas on leadership like Alice Sturgis' *The Standard Code of Parliamentary Procedure*, and the concepts of Dynamic Facilitation and Consensus Process, but nothing is being taught that brings people together to work effectively on projects of agreement.

Perhaps you're sold on RONR but we want to emphasize the fact that you can usually "Suspend the Rules," including those contained in RONR and supplant them with your own. You can make the change temporary or you can make it as permanent as rules that allow for their suspension can be. If, for example, you want to demand that to pass a motion it must be by consensus, you can place such a rule in your bylaws although Robert argues against it because he says it "becomes a form of tyranny."

We don't know when *Robert's Rules for Kids and Big Kids* (RRAK--Robert's Rules for All Kids) will be woven into the curriculum but there is plenty of evidence indicating it should be. The Texas Association of Student Councils (TASC) serves 1340 high school and middle school student councils. On their website, they say their parliamentary authority is "Robert's Rules of Order." The 11th edition of RONR says that no matter what edition of Robert's an organization's bylaws references, the 11th edition supersedes all previous editions. Nevertheless, the TASC bylaws were amended in 2012, 2013 and 2015. They have had time to change their bylaws to correctly reference *Robert's Rules of Order Newly Revised*. Is TASC unaware of the fact that all previous editions including the 10th are out of date? This, and so much more, is what we hope to fix.

PRESERVING AND ENRICHING THE DEMOCRATIC PROCESS

In a 1979 issue of the *Parliamentary Journal*, the American Institute of Parliamentarians published a speech by their president. Lucille Place wrote, "The Next Twenty Years:"

> Twenty years ago the first annual session of the American Institute of Parliamentarians was held in Chicago, Illinois… a handful of American citizens met for the purpose of preserving what Americans refer to as the democratic process.[1.5]

Preserving and enriching the democratic process is central to the publication of this book. During her speech, Place said, "… in the 30 years that I have actively supported and promoted the concept of the democratic process, I have been unable to convince one educational institution that it (education in parliamentary procedure) must be taught to every student if that student is to reach his or her greatest potential as a citizen of the world. "Where do individuals go to learn how to become parliamentarians? Must they continue to practice on the consumer?"[1.6]

As we write this book we have been unable to find a guide for teachers of students in grades K-12. There is a first version of this book, *Robert's Rules for Kids, a Guide to Teaching Children from Kindergarten to the 5th Grade: the Basics of Parliamentary Procedure*.[1.7] That book had a limited press run. This book builds on it, and we believe is a marked improvement.

Has anyone made any progress in teaching parliamentary procedure? Through advocacy, the answer is yes, but, there is still a need for this book and an organized, consistent approach, especially for younger students. In 1980, Dr. Aban Daruwalla who taught at Shelby State College in Memphis, TN, worked with AIP President Place in teaching parliamentary law in the public schools of Memphis. In *Parliamentary Journal* there was the following:"…every school-age child should be exposed to parliamentary procedure." Here are excerpts from Dr. Daruwalla's remarks:

> By now parliamentary procedure should have become a way of life in the schools of America. Instead, only a small percentage of the population is well versed in the subject. So it is high time for parliamentarians to come forward with their expertise and offer their assistance . . .

> The significant time given to parliamentary procedure by public school administrators is appalling. Few teachers are able to offer correct information on parliamentary procedure when they are asked to do so.[1.8]

Since 1980 three books, *RONR in Brief*, *The Idiot's Guide to Parliamentary Procedure* by Nancy Sylvester[1.9] and the *American Institute of Parliamentarians' The Standard Code*[1.10] have simplified the essential body of knowledge. The National Association of Parliamentarians has adopted a detailed *Body of*

Knowledge statement describing what professional parliamentarians need to know to function professionally. In 2015 the predecessor to this book, *Robert's Rules for Kids,* was published. But until now there hasn't been a guide that assists teachers at all grade levels in disseminating this information. Susan McElwain, a Houston-area educational consultant (and former student of Dr. Haun) was so moved by the remarks of Dr. Daruwalla that in the next issue of the *Parliamentary Journal*, she wrote "An Educational Rationale for the Inclusion of Parliamentary Procedure in the Elementary School Curriculum:"[1.11]

"To continue our democratic political process, we educators must realize the students in our classroom will be the voting citizens formulating the policies of the future. It is a grave responsibility that goes beyond simply achieving higher test scores. Parliamentary principles need to be introduced in the elementary classroom. They need to be developed over the schooling years in order to produce competent citizens. [This]. . . offers an opportunity to teachers to reemphasize the greatness that built America . . . to maintain the prestige of intelligence and the respect of nations."[1.12]

In *The Element,* a *New York Times* bestseller by Dr. Ken Robinson, he cites a school in central England that operates like a city.[1.13] They have a mayor and city government, a grocery store, TV station, and other key features of a city. The result has been higher academic evaluations (attendance, behavior and test scores) than ever before. One possibility for this is that students see the value of the subjects they are studying through their practical application.

We believe RRAK should be melded into existing curriculum so that students will build on their reading, writing, speech, math, history, psychology, philosophy, and sociology skills. Through this material they will have the opportunity to become actors and actresses, see its application to interior design, and even get some physical activity. There will be extensive opportunities for critical thinking.

At the very beginning, kindergartners will participate in the most rudimentary form of a committee meeting and then have the option of participating in a meeting following RONR for a Committee of the Whole. Much of the instruction should involve the Socratic Method. When appropriate, we believe students should learn how RONR evolved.

Our founding fathers did not have Robert's Rules when they were writing the Constitution. Instead Robert drew from the nation's founders. Using RONR as a resource, in Chapter 4 we invite middle and high school students to write a student government constitution or bylaws (the words are interchangeable). One part of it is the organization's objective or purpose. We suggest using The Preamble to the U.S. Constitution as an example since it is the highest order of word crafting. We also share the purpose of the United Nations that may have based its purpose on the Preamble.

Sometimes, in determining the outcome of a vote (but not a voice vote), math will come into play. After students develop a basic understanding of the fundamentals, they will employ critical thinking to make a motion. They will be asked to think critically when they evaluate two examples of children's literature.

Most of the people in organizations your authors have been affiliated with since 1962 have chosen to largely ignore RONR. Officers, as well as members, rarely participated in workshops designed to maximize its use. Is this why Putnam concluded that we are *Bowling Alone*?

Like Putnam, another Harvard professor, Daniel Goleman, also failed to recognize RONR. In his book, *Emotional Intelligence,* he writes, "I can foresee a day when education will inculcate students with certain essential competencies including cooperation."[1.14] But nowhere in his book does he reference RONR as an essential element of teaching cooperation. And yet, central to this process is majority rule, minority voice, and the orderly discussion of issues.

SPIRAL OF SILENCE

Then there is the question: Does "cooperation" mean compromise?

In 1974, German-born but partially University of Chicago-educated political scientist Elisabeth Noelle-Neumann postulated that people remain silent when they feel that their views are contrary to those held by the "majority."[1.15] Her theory suggests that people remain silent because they fear isolation and reprisal. Her theory, which we believe deserves serious consideration as you move forward in infusing RONR into your curriculum, is based on the idea that in certain situations we intuitively know the prevailing opinion. The spiral is advanced when someone in the perceived majority speaks. Noelle-Neumann argues that the minority feels intimidated and reluctant to voice their opinion. The reason is peer pressure.

The spiral effect activates a downward spiral. Fears build. The minority opinion holder never speaks. As a teacher, you have tremendous influence. You may take the role of the majority opinion holder. If you urge all of your students to think "outside the box," unique ideas may be forthcoming. This may be a significant antidote to the Spiral of Silence, assuming you believe it is virtuous to hear minority opinions. The focus of this book is learning RONR for now and for life. It remains to be seen if bucking the majority is a life-skill students develop and take with them or if they will ultimately succumb, for their own preservation, to the opinion of the "majority."

Spiral of Silence certainly played out in a university setting. At the end of a school year, the President of the Faculty Senate was asked why voting members of the faculty were so reluctant to engage in and sometimes challenge the university President. The response: We are faculty hoping to become department chairs, department chairs wanting to become deans, deans wanting to become vice presidents, and speaking up is perceived to be challenging authority. This puts advancement in jeopardy.

A Spiral of Silence exists because people feel vulnerable. They don't want to be under "attack." As long as this dominates society, change will be slow. Each of us has to decide what to do about it. We hope that the introduction of RONR into the curriculum is finally viewed as a tremendous asset to our society and the world, and not relegated to the downward Spiral of Silence.

Responding to the Spiral of Silence is not something to be addressed in a specific part of the curriculum or school day. *Habits of Mind* are also designed to be integrated into all aspects of the educational process and, really, into life. We feature them here because we believe they're a natural fit.

THE APPLICATION OF *ROBERT'S RULES OF ORDER NEWLY REVISED* TO *HABITS OF MIND*

The *Habits of Mind* were developed by Arthur L. Costa and Bena Kallick in 2000 as a set of 16 problem solving, life related skills, necessary to effectively operate in society and promote strategic reasoning, insightfulness, perseverance, creativity, and craftsmanship.[1.16] The understanding and application of these 16 Habits of Mind provide people with skills to work through real life situations that equip them to respond using awareness (cues), thought, and intentional strategies in order to gain positive outcomes.

Following each one of these paraphrased 16 Habits we have responded with ways to use RONR *and* RRAK *to apply, teach, and learn the habit.*

1. **Persisting**: Sticking to task at hand; follow through to completion; remain focused.
   Whether it's a project or an idea, in RONR it takes a majority vote, sometimes 2/3 and possibly even more to make something happen. This is not always easy; it takes persistence.
2. **Managing Impulsivity**: Take time to consider options; think before speaking or acting; remain calm when stressed or challenged; be thoughtful and considerate of others; proceed carefully.
   Sometimes in meetings, people lose their cool; they show anger and other emotions. In the extreme they may walk out or even quit if they are not getting their way. By managing impulsivity they may achieve positive outcomes.
3. **Listening with Understanding and Empathy:** Pay attention to and do not dismiss another person's thoughts, feeling and ideas; seek to put yourself in the other person's shoes; tell others when you can relate to what they are expressing; hold thoughts at a distance in order to respect another person's point of view and feelings.
   Discussion/debate is central to all aspects of RONR. In committees or small board meetings, the free flow of ideas, give and take, is central. By applying this habit of mind, the outcome should be better than one person's idea. The same is true in large meetings but there the dialogue is constrained. In both cases, though, this habit needs to be used continually.

4. **Thinking Flexibly:** Ability to change perspective; consider the input of others; generate alternatives; weigh options.
   Think about amendments or amendments to the amendment. When one is introduced, it is a demonstration of this habit.
5. **Thinking about Thinking (Metacognition):** Being aware of own thoughts, feelings, intentions and actions; knowing what I do and say affects others; considering the impact of your choices on yourself and others.
   No matter how you cut it, RONR is politics. In this environment people have factors at play that go unstated. Nevertheless, RONR puts participants in an environment where thinking about thinking happens all the time.
6. **Striving for Accuracy:** Check for errors; measure at least twice; nurture a desire for exactness, fidelity and craftsmanship.
   One of the first things that takes place in a meeting is a review of the minutes of the last meeting. Little mistakes, if not corrected, can have huge unintended consequences. Accuracy is tested all the time.
7. **Questioning and Posing Problems:** Ask yourself, "How do you know?"; develop a questioning attitude; consider what information is needed, choose strategies to get that information; consider the obstacles needed to resolve the problem.
   Is it when you are deciding how to vote on a motion or is it a desire to get something procedurally wrong right? Regardless, this habit is frequently in play.
8. **Applying Past Knowledge to New Situations:** Use what is learned; consider prior knowledge and experience; apply knowledge beyond the situation in which it was learned.
   People who belong to organizations bring different skills to the table. It may be that new people are trying to mesh with the old, experienced members. The "new kid on the block" may have a great deal to offer but unless there is a welcoming environment, as suggested by this habit, the knowledge will go unutilized. The opposite, new "kids" rejecting the wisdom of their elders can, without this habit, also be true.
9. **Thinking and Communicating with Clarity and Precision:** Strive to be clear and accurate; strive to be accurate when speaking and writing; avoid generalizations, distortions, minimizations and deletions when speaking and writing.
   Is it in debate, in the formation of a motion, or dealing with a procedural matter? Regardless this habit is in play. When people are clear, things operate smoothly. Participate in environments where this habit is necessary and one is likely to get better at it. Take a test where all you do is answer yes, no, or multiple choice questions and this habit will not exist.
10. **Gathering Data through All Senses:** Stop to observe what you see; listen to what you hear; take note of what you smell; taste what you are eating; feel what you are touching.
    In meetings, there will be times when participants have to make snap

decisions. If they use all their senses, they're likely to make a better decision.

11. **Creating, Imagining, Innovating:** Think about how something might be done differently from the "norm;" propose new ideas; strive for originality; consider novel suggestions others might make.
    Every time a new idea, a motion is presented, there is the opportunity to employ this habit. This is the antidote to calcified thinking. It's embedded in RONR.

12. **Responding with Wonderment and Awe:** Be intrigued by the world's beauty, nature's power and vastness for the universe; have regard for what is awe-inspiring and can touch your heart. Remain open to the little and big surprises in life you see in others and yourself.
    It happens when people are exposed to the best aspects of the environment. It happens when some great idea is presented for the first time. Think, for example, of the Preamble to the Constitution. The Preamble of the Constitution of the United States was written to chart the direction of our country. It reads: We the People of the United States, in Order to form a more perfect Union, establish Justice, insure domestic Tranquility, provide for the common defense, promote the general Welfare, and secure the Blessings of Liberty to ourselves and our Posterity, do ordain and establish this Constitution for the United States of America. *It was written in 1789 and is still inspiring. In an organization employing RONR, ideas that touch the heart happen all the time.*

13. **Take Responsible Risks:** Try something new and different; consider doing things that are safe and sane even though new to you; face fear of making mistakes or of coming up short and don't let this stop you.
    In an organization you have a limited amount of time, money and you don't want to jeopardize the reputation of the organization or the people in it. Nevertheless, there are times when you have to try something new. Of course it will occur when new officers are elected; it happens when new ideas in the form of motions are presented and passed; it happens when you vote to accept new members. RONR provides many opportunities to master this habit. Doing it successfully feels good.

14. **Finding Humor:** Laugh appropriately; look for the whimsical, absurd, ironic and unexpected in life; laugh at yourself when you can.
    Ugh. Do you have to go to another meeting? That won't be the attitude if humor is commonplace or at least present some of the time. Meetings are full of the unexpected. In fact, they can be the most unscripted part of a person's day.

15. **Thinking Interdependently:** Work with others and welcome their input and perspective; abide by decisions the work group makes even if you disagree somewhat; learn from others in reciprocal situations.
    Why have an organization or meeting? Synergy. There is strength in numbers when people are adept in applying this habit. Which comes first,

the habit or the opportunity to learn it? This question deserves an interdependent response.

16. **Remain Open to Continuous Learning**: Be open to new experiences; proud and humble enough to admit when you don't know; welcome new information on all subjects.
    While people in organizations should be true to their purpose, it's hard to imagine a situation where new things aren't happening. If one has not developed openness, they certainly will in an organization. That's our answer and we're STICKING TO IT.

THE FLEXIBILITY OF ROBERT'S, CARL SAGAN, AND CRITICAL THINKING

Robert's Rules of Order has been revised 10 times, most recently in 2011. It's used by organizations all over the world as an instrument that supplements an organization's written bylaws and rules of law.

Most people are first introduced to *Robert's Rules* while deeply immersed in a combative environment. If this were a game, it would be like throwing players into the middle of play with no basic understanding of the rules. Unfortunately, this happens, and it's a recipe for disaster. It's no wonder many people cringe at the thought of being part of a group that uses RONR.

The late Carl Sagan, a well-respected scientist, author, and philosopher, had an exchange with a caller on the National Public Radio (NPR) program *Science Friday*. Here's what they said:[1.17]

Sagan: Critical thinking [is] the demon-haunted word. My experience is that all children have an intact sense of wonder. That is, when I teach kindergarten or first grade, I have a room full of scientists; at least as far as wonder is concerned. They're not up on the skepticism quotient yet. That's fine; that's something that can be taught to them. By the time they get to high school, 12th graders, it's all gone; there are no follow-up questions. They're not listening to what their colleagues are saying. They're worried about how their questions will be received by their peers. Their minds have been turned off. The sense of wonder is almost gone. Something dreadful happens to students between 1st and 12th grade and it's not just puberty. The interest in science, which is there in 1st grade, is somehow beaten out of them by 12th grade. Part of that is that there are adults who are nervous about being asked penetrating questions by young people and so they give off-putting answers.

Caller: What can we do to teach critical thinking skills in the schools?

Sagan: Part of the problem is that you start teaching young people critical thinking and they'll start criticizing their political institutions and religious institutions and then the people in power will say, "Oh my God, what are we doing?"

Caller: What I want is to get the people in power to be the students in this project. I think the people in power have a vested interest to oppose critical thinking.

Sagan: Yes, they sure do. You see, if we don't improve our understanding of critical thinking, and develop it as kind of second nature, then we're just suckers ready to be taken by the next charlatan who ambles along, and there are lots of charlatans. There are lots of ways of gaining power and money by deceiving people who are not skilled in critical thinking. What you suggest is absolutely essential, but getting it done is very difficult since there are so many institutional impediments.

Sagan, like Putnam, appears to be unaware of the fact that interwoven into the study of *Robert's Rules* is critical thinking. *Robert's Rules* has been so marginalized in schools that both men appear oblivious to it. There are a few high school groups that apply it. These include the Future Farmers of America, Skills USA, Health Occupation Students of America, and Business Professionals of America. The Boy Scouts have a merit badge that includes it. Having been judges of competitions involving some of these groups, we have seen students thrown into the fray with minimal or no academic preparation.

By advocating the introduction *of RRAK* in kindergarten, this guide will make the competitive process and daily application of the rules smooth, seamless, and devoid of the pressure that commonly befalls people in organizations.

In a nationally syndicated column titled *Time to Take Teaching to a New Level*, published on November 21, 2010, Thomas Friedman quoted Tony Wagner, a Harvard-based education expert and author of *The Global Achievement Gap*. Wagner said, "There are three basic skills that students need if they want to thrive in a knowledge economy: the ability to do critical thinking and problem solving, the ability to communicate effectively, and the ability to collaborate."[1.18]

This sounds excellent except to address this problem Wagner postulates: "We need a new National Education Academy, modeled after our military academies, to raise the status of the profession and to support the R&D that is essential for reinventing teaching, learning and assessment in the 21st century."

In his February 8, 2014 nationally syndicated column, Ruben Navarrette Jr. wrote[1.19]: "Americans have become more resistant to considering different points of view… It's a harmful trend, and a clear recipe for atrophied thinking and a dysfunctional citizenry. We should never stop challenging our beliefs. Now that we know this is happening, there is only [the] question: How do we stop it?"

Unfortunately, neither Wagner nor Navarrette has the answer on their radar screen. The short-term answer, we believe, is a curriculum and school infused with RONR to get students excited about learning and to prepare them for civic engagement for the rest of their lives. When you implement this guide, you will see children who are engaged and animated while learning.

The principles embraced in this book have roots in the British Parliament,[1.20] the writings of Thomas Jefferson,[1.21] the *Rules of Order* developed by Henry M. Robert[1.22] and the successive authors/editions of his work. Some of the language in this book is adapted from the *Standard Code of Parliamentary Procedure* based on the work of Alice Sturgis and periodically updated by a review committee of the American Institute of Parliamentarians[1.23] in order to simplify the procedures for adults as well as children. For example, the motion *to consider* [a matter] *informally* is used instead of *committee of the whole and quasi-committee of the whole.*

Why don't we have more programs that enable persons to manage their meetings successfully? Why haven't we made a major impact in the schools? Certainly in secondary schools, youth organizations have developed that train many younger students through competitions to achieve these goals. But this only catches those with the time and instinct for these competitive extra-curricular programs. As far as we know, no one has developed teaching goals with identifiable outcomes that are grade specific from kindergarten through graduation. We think this book initiates that process.

When a child has only used fists or screaming to accomplish goals, the primary outcome is fights and/or tantrums. It is quite the revelation to become aware that people can band together and vote. In a democracy, this can lead to positive outcomes. In this book we provide tools for expression and action. These are skills that accompany the student into adulthood and can serve the individual well for the rest of his/her life.

Robert's Rules for Kids & Big Kids is rooted in the principles first set forth by Henry Robert, but for younger students the authors will generally use the more easily understood and contemporary language for motions and actions as permitted by Robert. *RONR*, p. 202.

LONG-RANGE GOALS

The goal in *RRAK* is to ultimately promote in both teachers and students these long-range goals to be completed by the time students graduate high school:

- Increase an understanding of the democratic process. Opinions affect our actions; voting is an important action.
- Motivate students to be an active part of the democratic process by appropriately voicing their opinions and actively, regularly voting. By graduation this should be an ingrained habitual response to issues.
- Demonstrate that parliamentary procedure is the best means for getting business transacted and making decisions in an orderly fashion while maintaining cooperation and harmony.

- Demonstrate that reasoned action is the logical and best alternative to bullying and emotionalism.

"The longer I live, the more I am satisfied of two things: first, that the truest lives are those that are cut rose-diamond-fashion, with many facets answering to the many-planed aspects of the world about them; secondly, that society is always trying in some way or other to grind us down to a single flat surface. It is hard work to resist this grinding-down action." ~ Oliver Wendell Holmes, *The Professor at the Breakfast-Table* 1859

CHAPTER 2: EARLY ELEMENTARY

"Children should be seen and heard."

Teaching Kindergartners

One morning out of the blue in a wonderful Houston bakery, the seed for teaching Robert's Rules to kindergartners was planted. A young girl wearing a beautiful multi-colored skirt with a bright yellow crinoline petticoat and bright, unmatched socks stood out.

"Who dressed your child?"
"She did," the mother said.
"How old is she?"
"Four."

Upon reflection, it dawned on us that if a four-year-old child could select such an incredible outfit, four-year-olds could weigh-in on which books should be in their school library. Four-year-olds are not too young to begin the process of learning democratic decision making.

Kindergarten is not too early to introduce children to the **gavel** of the presiding officer. Here is a real conversation with a four-year-old:

"Can I take your wooden hammer thing (pointing to the gavel in the picture) to school tomorrow?"

Fearing that the child wasn't beyond bopping another child on the head with it (she had seriously bitten the upper lip of a little boy who tried to kiss her), the adult asked,

"What are you going to do with it?"

"I'm the class president tomorrow."

"Wonderful," but persisting …"What does the class president do?"

"I hit the hammer-thing on the table and say, the meeting will come to order. Then people take turns talking—BUT they can't talk unless I call on them. When they finish talking, I say, "The meeting is over." I hit the hammer again and the meeting is over. Then we have story time."

"Yes, of course you can borrow the gavel." The conversation ended with the child learning the words "rap" and "gavel."

At age five, this child's group was learning orderliness, taking turns, and majority rule. Today, this same "child" is president of a not-for-profit foundation and a confident public speaker.

Early Education - Initial Focus on:

- **Courtesy during meetings.**
- **Handling one thing at a time.**
- **Doing things in good order.**
- **Keeping accurate records.**
- **Preserving the will of the majority; and being fair.**
- **Soliciting Ideas.**
- **Distilling Ideas.**
- **Voting.**

AN ALL-SCHOOL APPROACH

Most schools have a Student Council. Because they are elected, they are presumed to represent the entire student body. Of course they don't, but they can. We provide two ways to approach this. One approach is to have all students in the 4th grade team up, one on one, with all students in kindergarten and to have all students in the 5th grade team up, one on five, with all children in the 1st grade. We recognize that this is a complicated approach because it requires the participation of everyone. Nevertheless, we urge you explore the details of this model since it has application to the *Reading Rockets* exercise: Dictation on page 17.

Campus-wide Approach: Kindergarten. A 4th grader with a 2nd grade assistant teams up with a kindergartner to do the following:

1. All students involved put on nametags to identify them and to make it easy to remember names.

2. The 4th grader, soon to act in the role of a committee secretary, goes to the 2nd grade class to get an assistant who has been selected by the teacher. Both go to the kindergartner's class. All three go to the school library.

3. In the library, two kindergarten-appropriate books (*e.g.* one about lions and one about giraffes) will be examined by the kindergartner. [2.1]

4. The kindergartner's task is to recommend one of the two pre-approved books for the school library. This is a very simple introduction to *Robert's Rules* where the kindergartner is a committee of one. The kindergartner will share his or her thoughts with the 4th grader and 2nd grader. The 2nd grader is

learning what to do and will have this job in two years. The 2nd grader assists in the creation of the report, which is the recommendation of the kindergartner.

As is the case in all meetings, pen and paper or a computer tablet are vital. After the book is read by the kindergartner or 4th grader, or both, the following is a script of what might transpire. This is not the report:

> **4th Grader**: Which book do you think the school should buy?
>
> **Kindergartner**: The one about lions.
>
> **4th Grader**: Why?
>
> **Kindergartner**: Lions are pretty and strong.
>
> **4th Grader**: Did you like the pictures?
>
> **Kindergartner**: I thought they were great. Do you think the lady who took the pictures was safe? She sure got close to the lions.
>
> **4th Grader**: She must have been safe; she finished the book. Was the book too long?
>
> **Kindergartner**: No, it was good. The pictures were all different. I liked the story even though it was sad.
>
> **4th Grader**: This book will cost the school $24.
>
> **Kindergartner**: Is that a lot of money?
>
> **4th Grader**: I don't know. Do you think this book will last a long time?
>
> **Kindergartner**: I don't know. I think lots of kids will look at it.
>
> **4th Grader**: Why did you decide on this book?
>
> **Kindergartner**: The lion is king of the jungle. I like the way they look. I like them more than giraffes.

6. The 4th grader takes notes and shares the notes with their assistant. The kindergartner will then read what they wrote about the meeting and will either approve the report "as is" or suggest changes Here is an example of that report with the following key elements suggested by RONR, pp. 505-506:

   I. **The way the committee undertook its charge:**
   On April 10, 2016, 4th grade student John Doe and 2nd grade student Jane Smith escorted kindergartner Bob Johnson to the school library. There Bob looked at two picture books with the thought in mind, which one should the school purchase for the library. One book was about lions; the other book was about giraffes. He talked about both books. John took dictation.

II. The facts uncovered or information obtained:
Bob told Jane and John that that the lion was the king of the jungle, pretty and strong, and more interesting than a giraffe. By asking, Bob discovered that the lion book cost $24.
III. The findings or conclusions derived from the facts:
Bob concluded that more students would be interested in a book about lions than a book about giraffes.
IV. Recommendations:
He recommended (voted) that the school purchase the book about lions.

7. After all the meetings, the 4th grade Ambassadors share their reports with one another. A single representative selected by the 4th grade Ambassadors makes a report (described in #8 below) to the Executive Committee and then to the Student Council at a Regular Meeting. It is recommended that the 4th grade Ambassadors use a "Committee of the Whole" or one of its alternate forms as described in RONR, p. 530. This allows each presenter more time to speak and for others to ask as many pertinent questions as needed. Without the Committee of the Whole approach, only two statements per Ambassador would be permitted.

8. The Ambassadors should produce a numerical summary report, such as 10 students liked the lion book, and three the giraffe book. There also should be a consolidation of the ideas, such as "most kindergartners liked the lion story because lions roar." With this information, the Student Council may hear a better reason to buy the second-place book, instead of the one that received the most votes.

9. No matter what decision the Student Council makes, the kindergartners and the rest of the student body should be told which book was chosen over another. It is not necessary to provide an explanation.

This is the beginning exercise of teaching *Robert's Rules* to kindergartners. This is a representative form of democratic decision-making where they have tangible input.

As an alternative, the teacher assumes the role of the fourth grader. Each student will meet one-on-one with the teacher and go through the same exercise. When all the students have had an opportunity to read the two books and share their thoughts, the teacher will provide a summary report (a committee report) to the class. The class will discuss the report and pass on their recommendation to the Student Council.

Reading Rockets[2.2]
Early Elementary: K-1

The award-winning PBS program *Reading Rockets* received funding from the U.S. Department of Education from 2001 to 2012. Because it is a natural fit, we suggest the adaptation of some of its major concepts. For more information go to: http://www.readingrockets.org/audience/teachers

DICTATION

In your kindergarten class, when students are doing something that does not require your undivided attention, meet with each child. Give them two library books and ask them either to read them to you, read them with you, or listen to you read. After they finish, ask them to tell you their first or second choice for purchase for the school's library or for your class collection, and why. As they are doing this write down what they say. In this environment, you are playing the role of the committee's secretary and they are the other member of this committee.

Dictation offers a way for you to record a child's thoughts or ideas. Dictation provides a chance for you to model many writing behaviors including handwriting, matching sounds-to-letters to spell words, and sentence formation.

After you have written down their words, slowly read back to them what they have said. Then it's their turn. If necessary, you read a word and then they follow. If they can handle everything you wrote, let them. There are multiple goals here. Reading is one, but it is no more important than them expressing their ideas and receiving the validation that what they say counts. Let them know that you will be producing a report that will include input from every student in your class.

After you have received reports from every committee (each student), it will be your challenge to produce a report that shows: 1) how you undertook this charge; 2) what facts you uncovered; 3) the conclusions derived from the facts (how many students selected, in first place, a particular book); and, 4) recommendations.

When you read your report to the class, especially number 2 above, the facts you uncovered, ask the students who are hearing their words to raise their hands. Inform them in advance that they may hear their words more than once since other students may have said the same thing they said or something close to it. This should be a fun exercise with no right or wrong answers that build to the final vote.

If you don't have the money to purchase the book, perhaps the money can be raised. If not, since everyone has seen both books, let your students know that this is just an exercise. Also let them know that this is an introduction to Robert's Rules of Order.

Next, the class debates the recommendation from the report. Let them know in advance that, after the report is presented, they will have this opportunity. Unlikely as it may be, students may be swayed by substance in the report that causes them to vote for choice two. That is why the sheer numbers coming out of the committees of two may not determine the outcome.

Be sure to introduce the concept "I move that" followed by "book 1 (or 2) be the choice of our class." As the students debate this question, tell them that each student may only speak two times and for a maximum of 10 minutes unless they agree to a Special Rule that speeches are for some other time (longer or shorter). Don't get into the many other motions. This is just a starting point. We think it will be an exciting experience that you *must* retain and display in the form of minutes. The minutes contain the starting and ending time, date of the meeting, who called it to order, who made the motion (a student should be selected and prepared in advance), and the fact that the motion was approved or rejected after debate. The content of this debate, contrary to a Committee Report, is not included. Seconding the motion is unnecessary since the essence of it came from a committee of more than one person, the entire class.

Why *Reading Rockets* suggests the use of dictation:

- It allows students to watch an older student or adult writing using many conventions of writing, such as letter formation, punctuation, spacing between words, and more.
- Older students or teachers can model listening to a sound and writing the associated letter.
- It demonstrates that speech can be written down and read back.

EXAMPLES
Language Arts
The person doing the writing should model a clear sound-to-letter match. "We see a book about the moon. I'm going to write the word mmmmmmoon. What sound is at the beginning of moon? What letter makes that sound?" Encourage the child to read the sentence too.

After delivery of a consolidated report, debate on the motion begins. Now you are following the spirit of the *Reading Rockets'* suggestion.

Reading Rockets says, "Tell a group story. Sometimes called Language Experience Charts, group stories benefit from a shared class experience. Write down the children's ideas. If the book lends itself, prompt a sequence, 'What happened first? Then what?'" and so on. Record the sentences as the children dictate them. As you write, model a clear sound to letter match. If you read a book about the moon, write the word moon. "What sound is at the beginning of mmmmmmoon? What letter makes that sound?" When the story is finished, read the story aloud with the children. Read it several times, then ask the children if they would like to read it. Assuming the majority say yes, give everyone an opportunity to read. Later, copy the story on chart paper and display it in the classroom.

Social Studies
Teachers can follow this up with a read aloud exercise on a social studies topic. Teachers can write student dictations on chart paper that can be read by the whole class.

DIFFERENTIATED INSTRUCTION
For second language learners, students of varying reading skills, and for younger learners:

- Teachers should vary their expectations for the length of dictation based on a child's language and/or age. It's likely that the younger the child, the shorter the story. This exercise, however, can be repeated throughout elementary school.
- Strategies such as this enable children from other cultures to bring their different experiences into the classroom to share. Sharing dictations through whatever means will enrich the other students' experience.
- Dictations with the whole group in the form of a class story may serve to familiarize students with the strategy.

Research that supports this strategy
Some of the research done that involves dictation comes from a whole language perspective. Here's some of that research.[2,3]

- MacArthur, C. A., & Graham, S. (1987). Learning disabled students' composing under three methods of text production. *The Journal of Special Education*, 21(3), 22-42.
- Stahl, S. A., Miller, P. D. (1989). Whole Language and Language Experience Approaches for Beginning Reading: A Quantitative Research Synthesis. *Review of Educational Research*, 59, 87-116.
- Stauffer, Russell G. (1970). *The language experience approach to the teaching of reading*. New York: Harper & Row

The *Reading Rockets* approach has not, as far as we know, been used to teach Robert's Rules but there are many books available for the non- or beginning reader. Two that stand out are *Flotsam* and *Good Dog, Carl*.

Flotsam by David Wiesner is a 2007 Caldecott Award Winner about a camera that washes up on a beach and is found by an excited boy. He develops the film and views pictures the film contains. The last photo is of a girl holding a photo of a boy, holding a photo of a girl and so on. The boy photographs himself holding the print and then tosses the camera back into the sea, setting it on its journey towards the next recipient.

Good Dog, Carl by Alexandra Day is a fun book about mother who leaves her baby in the charge of a Rottweiler. With endearing illustrations and lots of humor, follow the baby's adventures during their eventful day.

Teaching 1st Graders

Much of what's involved in teaching *Robert's Rules* to 1st graders can build on what was taught to kindergartners or stand on its own. If students did not have the experience in kindergarten, that exercise can work here, perhaps with more challenging books. Here there is one significant difference. Instead of committees of one, now there will be committees of five. This is the process of reaching a final decision, purchasing a book for the school library. The process is:

SCENARIO

1. Students will continue to wear name tags. One 5th grader Ambassador, one 3rd grader who serves as assistant to the 5th grader, and five 1st graders who were selected at random will meet. The 5th grader gets the 3rd grader from his or her class, and both get the five 1st graders from their class. They all go to the school library. Pen and paper should be used for note-taking.

2. Three age-appropriate books of a similar genre, pre-approved by the Principal, will be examined by the 1st graders. The 5th grader Chairs the meeting and takes notes. The 3rd grade student assists.

3. The 1st graders share their thoughts about the books with the 5th grader. The 3rd grader also takes notes and eventually collaborates with the 5th grader in writing a report.

4. Each 1st grader will be asked to read and either approve or suggest changes to the notes. The first graders considered the following books:

    - *Molly the Pony* by Pam Kaster[2.1]
    - *Cowgirl Kate and Cocoa* by Erica Silverman[2.1]
    - *Rooster's Alarm*[2] by Ian Smith and Sean Julian[2.1]

The 1st graders are at a table. This is a hypothetical scenario:

5th Grader: I guess you have had enough time to look at the books. Is that true?

All Students Yes.

5th Grader: OK, let's hear from each of you as we go around the circle one time. After that you can speak as much as you want but you must raise your hand. I will recognize you.

Then the scenario continues:

Student #1: I liked *Molly the Pony* the best. It was a true story. I like stories that are real.

Student #2: *Rooster's Alarm* was funny. The other books were too serious.

Student #3: *Cowgirl Kate and Cocoa* is about a girl and her horse. Lots of kids want horses. This story shows they can take care of a horse.

Student #4: Let's raise the money and get all three books. They were all good.

Student #5: I didn't like *Rooster's Alarm*. It was silly.

Student #1: My cousin lives in Louisiana where *Molly the Pony* took place. It's close to here. We should get a book that happened near here. We can only get one book.

Student #4: OK, let's decide on one book.

Student #3: *Molly the Pony* is about ponies not horses. They're not horses but the back cover says it's a story about a horse. That's confusing.

Student #5: May I see that?

Student #3: See.

Student #5: You're right.

Student #1: I changed my mind. Student #3 thinks we should have a book about horses. I want a book about them too. Everybody can read about this horse if we do.

Student #2: *Cowgirl Kate and Cocoa* has funny parts too. And it's about horses. I think it is the best book.

5th Grader: Do you have any more ideas or are you ready to vote?

All Students: We're ready.

5th Grader: How many of you want *Cowgirl Kate and Cocoa*? Now let me be clear we are voting for the library to buy *Cowgirl Kate and Cocoa*. How many of you want *Cowgirl Kate and Cocoa*?

All Students: Me, Me, Me, Me, Me.

5th Grader: It's unanimous. That's five votes for *Cowgirl Kate and Cocoa*. *Cowgirl Kate and Cocoa* is the winner.

NOTE: Students must keep in mind that when one person is talking, everyone else listens. Before the vote, it's important to repeat the "motion" three times (as seen in the example above) so everyone knows what he or she is voting on.

The final results are announced.

NOTE: The same approach used by 4th grade Ambassadors should be used here with the 5th grade Ambassadors.

Part of the consolidated report to the Student Council should be numerical. For example, 50 students voted for *Cowgirl Kate and Cocoa*, 24 for *Rooster's Alarm* and 26 for *Molly the Pony*.

3rd grade and 5th grade Ambassadors should consolidate all the ideas because the Student Council may hear a great idea about the 2nd or 3rd place book and decide to recommend another book over the one with the most votes.

More than one vote may be necessary. The approach is called "filling blanks." If no book gets a majority, the book with the lowest number of votes is dropped and there is a second vote. This same approach is used when there is a vote on three or more things, issues or people. Frequently people are intimidated by the thought of using "filling blanks," but if a motion passes to "create a blank" and it is filled with multiple items, the result is fair–the will of the majority, not a plurality, determines the outcome.

The entire student body should be informed of the decision, but it is not necessary to give the reasons behind it. There may be many reasons and it would be impracticable if not unlikely that the student council could give them all.

The 1st graders have begun to learn how to work in a committee and have taken the next step in learning how representative decision-making works.

ALTERNATIVE 1ST GRADE APPROACH

An alternative is for the 1st grade teacher to assume the role of the secretary. In both the kindergarten and 1st grade classes, a summary of all the reports is shared with the class. The kindergarten report might indicate that more students selected the book about lions than giraffes but something in the report, perhaps that giraffes are less violent, might strike a chord with the students. As a result, they may vote for the giraffe book even though in the committees, the lion book received the most votes.

In the 1st grade class, repeat the *Reading Rockets* exercise with one significant change: Initially, have five students meet with you. Select three age- appropriate books. The same seven rules designed for small boards and committees apply (see below). Because they're easy to learn—and so often misused—we suggest that you consider introducing additional forms of voting. If the first vote was a voice vote, introduce raising one's hand (not both hands) or standing. While it's unlikely that in a group of five that you will need to have anything other than a voice vote, we suggest that you consider playing around with close voice votes where a re-count is necessary. Let the students know that when there is no doubt, a time-consuming counted vote is not appropriate.

After the entire class has reported in groups of five, students will learn from their secretary (the teacher) the total number of votes for each book from each group.

PROCEDURES IN SMALL BOARDS AND COMMITTEES

In the 10th edition of RONR published in 2000, the authors explained in some detail rules for committees. These rules are the same in the 11th edition.

RONR's rules for boards with 12 people or less and committees are very simple:

1. Instead of standing to obtain the floor to speak, members may raise their hand. They also may remain seated while making motions or speaking.

2. Motions do not need to be seconded. Any member of a committee can place a motion before the committee.

    NOTE: RONR encourages ideas and provides a means for sharing them. As long as the person offering the idea stays within the scope of the committee, they are permitted to do so. Essentially, it's brainstorming that is designed to lead to a positive outcome.

3. There are no limitations on the number of times members may speak to a motion, but motions to close or limit debate are *"generally not allowed (RONR)."*

    Note: The 11th edition of RONR addresses what happens when someone abuses this privilege or is just speaking to delay action by the committee. The Chair can refuse to call on this person, the committee can vote to remove this person from the meeting, or initiate the process of removing them from the committee.

4. Informal discussion of a subject is permitted when no motion is pending.

    NOTE: In all committees, you are permitted the luxury of informality because it allows time to explore an issue in every way possible before developing a motion. The result is a motion that was not generated in haste.

5. When an idea is perfectly clear to all present, a vote can be taken without a formal motion being presented.

> NOTE: Once the idea is voted on, a clear description of the idea or motion should be produced so everyone in the organization and outsiders are clear on what is being proposed. Without clarifying the motion, the committee would be unclear about what will be done.

6. The Chair need not stand while putting questions to a vote.

> NOTE: In all groups, it's useful to have a Standing Rule addressing the seating arrangement. If possible, try to arrange the room so everyone can see the faces of their fellow members. It is essential that you arrange the room so that the Chair can see everyone and everyone can see the Chair.

7. The Chair may speak and vote on all questions.

> "The difference between success and failure is doing a thing nearly right and doing it exactly right."
> – Edward Simmons

CHAPTER 3: MIDDLE & LATE ELEMENTARY

"If all you have is a hammer, then everything looks like a nail."
— Aesop

This popular saying re-emerged late in the 20th century. It also came into use when "bullying" gained new proportions as students, unable to find adequate words and resources to express themselves when faced with ostracism and insecurity were unable to adequately express ideas and defend themselves against peer pressure and bullies. Many got into fights. In extreme but rare instances, others took handguns to school and used them. Unable to express their ideas or find adequate social support, many children found school to be a source of misery rather than a place to learn.

FOR THE TEACHER

This was further compounded by generations of parents who were reared in the United States as well as elsewhere in the world with the mantra that "children should be seen but not heard." A child who is back-handed by a parent for expressing a different opinion or viewpoint soon learns to keep silent. That parent is not going to defend their child at school or confront a teacher about a school policy.

Some parents did find the skill and freedom to be outspoken. These "helicopter parents" addressed some problems but created new self-centered problems in the process. A judge in Texas accepted "affluency" as an excuse for illegal teenage behavior. The defense was that the young man was so pampered by his family that he had no respect or concern for the rights and feelings of others.

In contrast, some schools recognize the value of teaching the democratic process:

In Utah at Layton Christian Academy, teacher Mrs. Cheryl Sligar, created an Elementary School Student Council that focuses on altruistic projects while helping build future leaders. We would like to see programs like this intentionally structured into the curriculum with parliamentary concepts applicable to grade level. [3.1]

The Texas Association for Student Councils, some 1340 member schools strong, references RONR as their authority as they seek to develop in students "leadership abilities" and to promote democracy." We'd like to see the adoption of this book or any organized sequential curriculum to specifically achieve goals.[3.2]

A K-12 school in New York, the Brooklyn Free School, teaches students to take full responsibility for their own education. This school is operating under the democratic principles of "direct democracy, inclusion, diversity and equality[3.2]," Until approached by us their former Executive Director, Allen Berger, said: "We just do it." Now they have these democratic decision-making skills and will for the rest of their lives.[3.3]

We suggest the following:

Teaching 2nd and 3rd Graders

During kindergarten and 1st grade, students received an introduction to RONR. They experienced a committee of one in kindergarten and a committee of five in the 1st grade. If the approach involved 4th and 5th graders facilitating the conversation/chairing the meeting, they also saw 2nd and 3rd graders assisting. Now that they are in the 2nd or 3rd grade, they'll be ready to get into the meat of RONR. We think this is a good time to introduce the vocabulary of RONR.

In boards of 13 or more members and in general membership meetings business basically begins with a motion. Motion, we suggest, should be the first vocabulary word students learn. While there are exceptions, motions generally require the next word students should learn: second. This should be followed by interrupt, debate, amend, vote required, majority, and even two-thirds (two out of three if this concept is easier for the students), and reconsider. These are words that come up throughout RONR but especially when one is talking about a Main Motion.

There are five categories of motions; **Main, Subsidiary, Privileged, Incidental,** and **Restorative** or **Bring Back**. The Main Motion is the lowest in rank. It stands alone but is the most influential. Working from the bottom up the seven subsidiary motions come next. These are followed by five privileged motions, 27 incidental motions and five bring back/restorative motions. Drawing from the glossary of parliamentary terms on pages 63-67, you can introduce these terms over the course of the next two years (2nd and 3rd grade). If your students are not assisting 4th and 5th graders in a campus-wide initiative with kindergarteners and 1st graders, they can meet in small committees with you to explore ideas that will be developed into motions and delivered to the Student Council.

Specific Outcomes: Grades 4-5

By the time students complete elementary school they should have a mastery of these concepts:

1. Majority rule is fair. [More than half is a majority.]
2. Everyone has the right to be heard (see Spiral of Silence, p. 5).
3. Things should be done in proper order. Understanding the precedence of motions is analogous to setting goals and keeping priorities straight.
4. Understanding differences between small groups and large organizations and how they work. The larger groups are, the more centralized (and procedure oriented) they need to be.
5. Students can become comfortable in chairing small committees and working with larger groups including presiding.
6. *Robert's Rules of Order Newly Revised* (RONR) and this book provide the information students need.

Unless the study of this subject is adopted campus-wide, time for this project will vary from one classroom to another and from one day to another. It will be up to you, the teacher, to determine how much time you can invest in helping students understand and develop skill in implementing these principles. We know that for most of you, your schedule is tight. We encourage you to stress these principles as part of other lessons. Consider it as a challenge to your creativity to use our suggestions. For example:

Language Arts: When writing sentences, have students write "motions."

   A. Phrased as a Main Motion:

   1. *We need new trash cans in the gymnasium* becomes: "I move that a committee of two students be appointed to contact the principal about purchasing new trash cans for the gymnasium."

   2. *We need healthier food choices in the cafeteria* becomes: "I move that this class petition for healthier food choices in the cafeteria."

   3. *We should select representatives to encourage the principal to permit a special school-wide celebration for Cinco de Mayo* becomes: "I move that we select three representatives to meet with the principal and encourage having a school-wide celebration of Cinco de Mayo."

   4. *Because Thomas Jefferson's birthday is April 10, we should celebrate April as Parliamentary Procedure month* becomes: "I move that this class petition the principal to celebrate April as Parliamentary Procedure month because Thomas Jefferson's birthday is April 10."

   B. Phrased as a resolution:

A resolution might be appropriate and fun; for example, as a "resolution:"

   1. "Whereas, all students in the class have had perfect attendance for the past week; and,

   2. Whereas, all students scored 85% or higher on their last weekly quiz, be it therefore RESOLVED: That on Friday, we have a popcorn party; and, be it further resolved that

Arts: 1. Students wear their silliest cap/hat for the party; and that

Math: 2. Each student contributes 25 cents toward purchase of popcorn."

Spelling: (See the glossary at the end of Chapter 5 for more spelling words.)

Language: Build on the 2nd and 3rd grade vocabulary words.

    Beginning: recess, fair, vote, turn, table, limit, gavel, mace

    Intermediate: majority, minority, adjourn, minutes, president, commit, postpone

    Advanced: privilege, rescind, reconsider, incorporation, statutes, previous

Mathematics:

A *majority* does not have to be a whole number; it may be a fraction. Use multiplication to determine more than half. Several motions including close debate/move the previous question, rescind, and amend something previously adopted require a 2/3 vote. Use multiplication to determine 2/3. Talk about how this can affect outcomes. Perhaps the fastest and easiest way to determine a 2/3 vote is to double the "no" votes and compare them to the "yes" votes.

In condominium associations, voting is determined by the percentage of square footage the member owns. The owner of the penthouse gets a "bigger" say in decisions than does the owner of an efficiency unit. This can lead to some very complicated math problems.

Communication: Do the exercises orally rather than as written exercises.

Social Studies: Do exercises orally.

    A. If any parent is an officer in an organization, have them visit the class and describe their responsibilities and experiences.

    B. Students could research the fascinating history of The Mace.

    C. Another research project: Maybe a history fair project. How many kinds of gavels are there? Where is the largest gavel in the world?

    D. Ask students to research and report on the history of Henry Martyn Robert.

COGNITIVE, EMOTIONAL, OR BEHAVIORAL RESPONSES

When you were in college, did you have to articulate your teaching philosophy? Did it change after you actually got in the classroom? Dr. Haun's philosophy did. She started out believing that learning was basically the positive outcome of paying attention, doing your reading or other homework and reviewing for tests. While this is important and often true, there is so much more to it. It's amazing how graduate courses in educational psychology can help. Even Aristotle recognized that speakers could use attention factors (activity, novelty, suspense, movement, color, physical objects/visual aids, *etc.*) to hold attention, clarify, and make messages more interesting. Examples–whether described or actual physical items (like a gavel)–brought the subject into a more meaningful cognitive realm.

Students of persuasive speaking quickly learn that audiences will have either negative, neutral or positive responses to a message. Even positive responses vary in strength and intensity and fall into basic categories of cognitive, emotional or behavioral responses. We have to understand in order to feel and, if we feel strongly, we are more likely to overtly respond. September 11, 2001 is a prime example of this phenomenon. Within hours some people felt so strongly that they packed immediately, drove to New York City and joined the recovery effort. Others sent money and/or stood in hot weather in long lines to donate blood to save lives. These are behavioral responses. Others watched the news and wept (emotional but no measurable behavior change) and others just shared the news as changes occurred (a cognitive response). Such were "opinion leaders" or "point people" but not much besides information changed for them internally. This phenomenon has been labeled "narcotizing dysfunction." These folks watch the news for hours or sit through hours of meetings but never respond with meaningful action. We believe that developing parliamentary prowess will be empowering for people to overtly and meaningfully respond to issues.

ACTIVITIES FOR LATE ELEMENTARY—GRADES 4-5

Any Google search of Bloom's cognitive levels will produce a myriad of models of his learning domains with updates and revisions by subsequent writers.[3,4] Two of Bloom's Domain Taxonomies (Cognitive and Emotion-Based) are particularly relevant to our goals:

Knowledge-based or cognitive domain

    6. Creating

    5. Evaluating

    4. Analyzing

    3. Applying

    2. Understanding (comprehending)

    1. Remembering

It is fundamental for students to (1) remember what they have heard–new terms, concepts, definitions, principles. Such activities are measured when you ask them to list, state, identify, label, name: Who? What? When? Where? Why? How? This includes rules for activities, *etc.* (2) Comprehension or understanding of what they are remembering is important (and it is why we will not recommend esoteric words, motions, and concepts). We have more important things to do. We can assess this learning when we ask them to explain or interpret (e.g. bylaws), predict, infer, give examples or paraphrase. (3) You will know students are really "getting the ideas" when they are able to use/apply vocabulary and concepts in class activities/exercises. They will be at level (4) when they can use the chart of ranking motions and preside over a meeting or when they can watch their Student Council perform and analyze the behaviors they observe. Students have reached level (5) when they can successfully identify strengths and weaknesses of self or others in performance and outcomes. You'll know they are at level (6) when they are writing scripts, creating scenarios and adopting motions they can take into the real world.

Late Elementary Kids can compare:

- The law of the land.
- Articles of Incorporation
- Constitution
- Bylaws
- Standing Rules

Late elementary kids can ask their parents for copies of their renters' or homeowners' deed restrictions; divide into groups/committees to compare; and, report back to the whole class. This is both a reading comprehension as well as compare and contrast/analysis activity.

> "The secret of getting ahead is getting started."
> — Mark Twain

The Affective Domain (emotion-based)

5. Characterizing

4. Organizing

3. Valuing

2. Responding

1. Receiving

Why do we include the affective/emotional domain? Because ultimately, all human behavioral responses are linked to emotional responses. Emotional response is based on what we know and believe–which is a cognitive domain. We want a behavioral response from students. What we are about is more than a recall test to see how many fancy new words a student has learned. Feeling pleased and confident with oneself is an emotional response; just being knowledgeable is not enough. We want students to perceive value in this new learning. We want a behavioral response. We want students to use their parliamentary skills to participate in committee meetings they run themselves; to participate in and lead Student Council meetings, and ultimately to have these skills for the rest of their lives.

Translated into our domain taxonomy, students need to receive pleasant invitations to opportunities, be capable of response, value those responses to the extent that they organize their positive responses so that they become habits that automatically characterize their behavior such as the ability to readily walk to a microphone, properly word a Main Motion, and speak articulately in defense of it or pick up a gavel and Chair a meeting naturally and comfortably.

Thanks to Ivan Pavlov and others, we know the value of positive conditioning. "Rewards" are important and will vary among groups based on skills developed at different age levels. For second graders, popcorn on Fridays may be a sufficient "reward." In high school it may be competition as a HOSA (Health Occupations Student Association) team where winning the state championship and placing at nationals are the goals. There are several excellent competitive high school level programs.

As teachers of young children, your experience will serve well in determining which exercises fit best with which students. Some abstract principles may not work until the student has achieved Piaget's "reversibility." However, we know that the younger the child is, the more easily a "foreign language" is mastered. To many adults, Robert's "rules" are akin to a foreign language. This simply reinforces to your authors that the experiences we advocate in this book are best integrated into the curriculum from early age. As student skills gain precision, so increases the student's ability to protect the rights not only of self, but likewise of the majority, the minority, and the absentees.

Skills Model

Precision

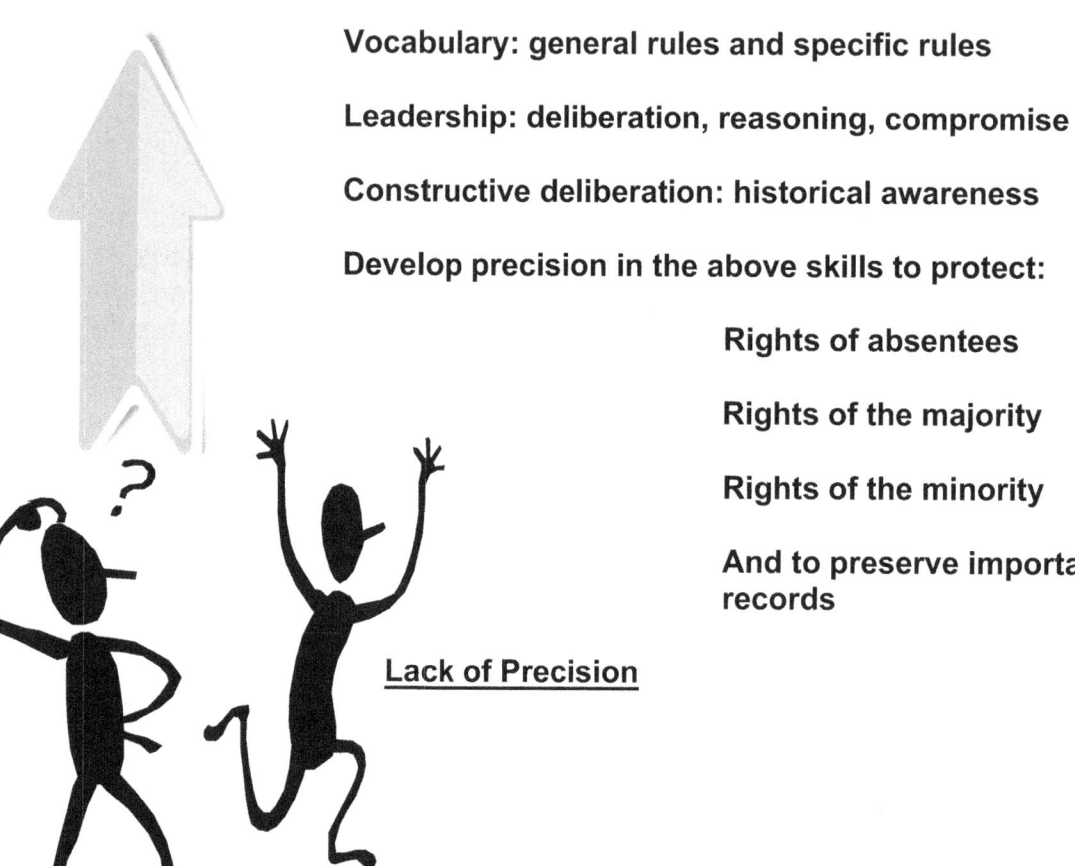

Vocabulary: general rules and specific rules

Leadership: deliberation, reasoning, compromise

Constructive deliberation: historical awareness

Develop precision in the above skills to protect:

       Rights of absentees

       Rights of the majority

       Rights of the minority

       And to preserve important records

Lack of Precision

What's Your Opinion? Why?

Students need to become comfortable expressing ideas and opinions in a group situation. This is fundamental to debating issues when discussing the pros and cons of a motion. Stay alert for discussion topics that are appropriate for your students. Start with simple, often campus-related topics and build toward bigger social issues and real world decisions.

You might try the following in response to bullying:

Bullying is directly related to our freedom of expression. Discussion should include why people attempt to bully in meetings, talk/shout down their opponents, *etc.* [**Clue**– They lack resources to discuss fairly and reach compromise through amendments. They need to be enabled with democratic tools. Without resources, they are primed for lose/lose situations. This may be the resource that produces a win/win outcome.]

or

Discuss a famous quotation of your choosing. *e.g.*

> It is reported that great people talk about ideas, average people talk about things, and little people talk about other people.
> — Eleanor Roosevelt

Common Stages in Group Process:

Aubrey Fisher said the stages are[3.5]

1. **Orientation**–What are we (the group) doing? What are we supposed to find out?

2. **Conflict**–What is the best course of action? The best interpretation *etc.*? What are the pros and cons?

3. **Emergence**–The best ideas rise to the top as the focal point of a discussion and plans emerge.

4. **Convergence**–A plan of action supported by the majority takes form as the group approaches consensus on a decision.

5. **Reinforcement**–Affirm the decision of the group as the best course of action.

John Dewey said groups go through these stages:[3.6]

1. Identify the **Problem**/Need;

2. Establish **Criteria** for a Workable Solution;

3. List **Possible Solutions**.

4. Select a **Plan of Action** (Advantages/Disadvantages.)

5. **Implement** the Plan.

PROBE: Can you think of a group that needs new or updated rules? Do you have ideas for what those rules might be?

Did you know that John Quincy Adams wrote the rules for the formation of the U.S. Navy? It is unlikely that he could even start to imagine the amendments that would be made to his document as it expanded over the next 250 years.

Methods of Voting

Put these terms in **a Word Search.** Have a discussion about which is most desirable under different circumstances. (See the glossary for definitions.)

Voice (Vote)	Bullet (Voting)
Show of Hands (Vote)	Written (Ballot)
Standing (Vote)	Secret (Ballot)
Counted (Vote)	Preferential (Ballot)
Proxy (Voting)	

Any theme related to vocabulary words can be used.

MATH EXERCISE:

Sample Teller's Report–This makes a good math exercise; change the number of votes cast and rework the problem.

Number of Votes Cast	100
Number Necessary for Election	51 (majority)
Mr. Adams received	14
Ms. Smith received	55
Ms. Jones received	30
Illegal votes:	
Mr. SpongeBob (ineligible)	1

x_____ Signature, Chief Teller

*NOTE: Blank ballots are not counted.

Who wins?

A Simple Set of Bylaws

FOR THE TEACHER:

Bylaws can be very simple yet thorough. RONR calls for nine articles. Since this is only a sample, we encourage teachers and classes to follow Article IX and to amend them as they see fit. Complexity can be added for age and understanding. See the Appendices for two other examples of bylaws.

Bylaws are the governing documents of an organization. Help younger students understand that groups, like individuals, must follow the rules–federal, state and local laws. Schools, churches, neighborhoods (their parents in homeowner associations, *etc.*) all have laws/rules that they must follow. It's all part of an orderly and safer society. Students can discover how bylaws govern many organizations and compare and contrast different bylaws.

Sample Bylaws
Mrs. Curry's Cougars

Article I. Name: Mrs. Curry's Cougars.

Article II. Purpose: To learn the basics of parliamentary procedure through class activities and by practicing majority rule and listening to students who don't have the same opinion I do.

Article III. Members: The students enrolled in Mrs. Curry's class.

Article IV. Officers: These individuals shall be elected by the class but may be replaced by other members of the class so everyone is given leadership skills or, if necessary, by the teacher.

    A. A Class President who shall work with the teacher to conduct class meetings.
    B. A Class Vice President who shall work with the president and the teacher to conduct class meetings.
    C. A non-voting adult Secretary who shall take minutes at meetings of Mrs. Curry's Cougars.
    D. A Class Treasurer who shall work with the teacher (or the teacher) to report what is happening with class funds.

Article V. Meetings: Class, Executive Committee and Committee meetings shall be held at times designated by the teacher.

Article VI. Executive Committee: The Class President, Vice President, Secretary (Non-Voting) and Treasurer [or] teacher.

    A. With the teacher's approval, the Executive Committee shall meet upon the call of a majority of the voting members of this committee. When they meet, it shall be up to the teacher to determine if the class will observe or work independently.
    B. All members of the Executive Committee may be replaced at any time by either the teacher or a majority vote of the class.
    C. Since replacements can happen at any time, it is advisable for members of the class to observe as frequently as possible.
    D. The Executive Committee should meet for at least 30 minutes, once per week.

Article VII. Committees: There shall be at least one committee. If it's only one, it will be the class meeting as a Quasi Committee of the Whole. It shall meet upon the call of the teacher, a majority of the Executive Committee, or a majority of the class. The teacher shall have veto power.

A. The teacher or the Class President shall chair these committee meetings.
   B. Other committees may be established for specific projects. These committees will meet upon call of the Executive Committee. The Class President appoints committee members and the Chairs.
   C. Committees should meet for at least 30 minutes, one time per week.

Article VIII. Parliamentary Authority: *RONR*

   A. The teacher shall serve as the class parliamentarian and offer advice to the Class President.
   B. *Robert's Rules of Order Newly Revised (RONR)* shall govern the class in all cases to which they apply.

Article IX. Amendments: These bylaws may be amended at any time by a majority vote and the approval of the teacher.

"Education is the most powerful weapon you can use to change the world."
— Nelson Mandela

CHAPTER 4: MIDDLE AND HIGH SCHOOL

PHILOSOPHY

Our philosophy has not changed as we reach out to older, more mature students. We are simply ready to implement Bloom's higher cognitive domain. You should expect higher analytical skills from students as well as more empathy, suggesting a different level of maturity in social as well as cognitive skills. In Chapter 7, we provide a parliamentary script that can be used several times as students change characters and identify with different roles.

In his social learning theory, Albert Bandura recognized that we learn through information acquisition (we read the instructions), direct experience (we get thrown in the deep end of the swimming pool), role-playing (easily done by playing out scripts), and modeling (imitation of great speakers, artists, presiding officers). The teacher or advanced student who can demonstrate expertise in handling motions provides an important teaching tool.[4.1]

The various competitive events available to some high school students go beyond the reading of scripts and call for the individual to develop a personal repertoire of skills for "any occasion."

Theorist Susan Shimanoff has developed a theory that stresses the importance of rules to human beings. This clarifies for us why the rules that Robert developed are important and in many cases feel so natural to us.

Shimanoff observed:[4.2]

1. People choose courses of action to accomplish their intentions.
2. Social behavior is structured and organized.
3. Rules are the social mechanism through which social action is organized.

She further observed:

1. Rules must be follow-able. (A rule that one must be able to personally fly to the moon and back as a condition of membership is impossible to follow).
2. Rules are prescriptive (they tell us what to do).
3. Rules are contextual; that is, what is appropriate in one context may not be in a different situation; *e.g.*, consider a small committee meeting compared to a national political convention of delegates.
4. Rules specify appropriate behavior. RONR clarifies when it is acceptable to interrupt another speaker, when a motion requires a second to move forward, when a speaker should rise and formally address the Chair, and so on. These are appropriate behaviors for a fair and orderly meeting.[4.2]

HIGH EXPECTATIONS
Specific Goals: Middle School & High School
1. Develop expertise and confidence in actively presiding and participating in meetings.
2. Develop expertise in all parliamentary terminology.
3. Where possible, become an active part of student competitions in parliamentary procedure such as Skills USA and Health Occupations Students of America competitions (local, state and national).
4. Become an active member of a professional parliamentary organization such as National Association of Parliamentarians (www.parliamentarians.org) and/or American Institute of Parliamentarians (www.aipparl.org). Pursue full certification as a professional parliamentarian.

BYLAWS

Bylaws are the foundation of an organization. If people come together to start an organization, the first thing they should do is create a *draft of the bylaws*.

As part of this process, the group should discuss the organization's goals.

Later, as the group size increases, a Bylaws Committee should write formal bylaws to be considered, possibly amended, and then adopted by the group members.

Failure to develop and follow good bylaws is a recipe for disaster.

The bylaws below are a modified version of the sample bylaws found in *Robert's Rules of Order Newly Revised*.[4.3] The nine articles (**N**ame, **O**bjective, **M**embership, **O**fficers, **M**eetings, **E**xecutive Committee, **C**ommittees, **P**arliamentary Authority, and **A**mendments) are essential to an organization.

An easy way to remember these articles is to use the mnemonic, or the first letter of each part. **NO MOME CPA**

Follow this approach in forming your student government:

1. Have a committee of about 20 students, including "good" and "bad" kids, make recommendations to the Principal to adopt the following bylaws by filling in the blanks.

2. Have the students vote on each section and then on the whole. The students are functioning in a way that is like the way the U.S. Congress passes laws but please note: Congress does not follow RONR. Some key exceptions are: no filibustering and no right of the Chair to veto legislation.

3. In some schools, the Principal acts like the President and vetoes or signs motions.

SAMPLE: SIMPLE MINUTES

Minutes are the roadmap for every organization. They tell everyone where you've been and where you're headed. It is the responsibility of everyone to read minutes and to offer, when necessary, corrections. There is a cardinal rule: Minutes, unlike committee reports (see below), should report what was done, not what was said.

**Big Kids Klub Minutes
Association of Parliamentarians
February 8, 2018**

The meeting was called to order on Thursday, February 8, 2018, at 8:32 a.m. by President Molly Munchkin in the classroom of Mrs. Teacher. A quorum (of more than 12 people) was present.

Reports

Jerry Jones read the report for Treasurer Laura Lane who was unable to attend:

Beginning Balance (on January 11, 2018)	$51.13
Income (flower sale)	20.00
Disbursements	0.00
Balance on February 8, 2018	$ 71.13

The report was filed for audit.

The minutes of the January 11, 2018 meeting were read and approved as corrected. *[The correction goes in the minutes being corrected.]*

Program

The program was presented by Renee Rose on Precedence of Motions and used group activities. Participants received prizes.

New Business

Will Works moved that we discuss meeting in the summer months in an informal committee for 10 minutes. Laura Lane raised a Point of Order that no second was made. The point was well taken. The motion was seconded. Dennis the Menace raised a Point of Order that a Main Motion must be made before an informal committee can be considered. The point was well taken.

The meeting adjourned at 8:50 a.m. *[This is assumed to be the normal time for adjournment. It is a privileged motion and, as such, the name of the maker of this motion not does not belong in the minutes.]*

COMMITTEE REPORTS

Committee reports contain: 1) How the committee arrived at its results; 2) The information it obtained; 3) The meaning of what it found out; and; 4) What they decided, and if they decided to move forward the motion or resolution they wish to make.

DISCIPLINARY PROCEDURES

This is a story about Furr High School. This is what occurred prior to the introduction of RONR. It was before they began the process of starting a student government. It is how Restorative Justice (RJ) and RONR complement each other.

Dr. Bertie Simmons was retired on the calamitous day of September 11, 2001, when two airplanes crashed into the World Trade Center in New York, a third hit a section of the Pentagon, and a fourth crashed into an empty field in Pennsylvania.

Dr. Simmons had been asked a number of times to return to work and repeatedly said no. Then a personal calamity struck. Her precious granddaughter, Ashley Fendley, was killed in a skiing accident. Ashley was going to change the world. The following year, Dr. Simmons decided she had to fill this void.

Gang activity was a frequent occurrence at Furr High, a school that is located near the Houston Ship Channel, about 10 miles east of downtown Houston. Some might think that this was a demotion for someone who had been a District Superintendent but not Dr. Simmons. She quickly discovered that the school was dysfunctional, and that no one was effectively addressing the problem.

Her first move was to identify the gang leaders. She invited all of them to her office for a no-holds barred heart-to-heart talk. She asked them if they realized that they were throwing away not only their lives but also the lives of others. Their response, "The education here; you're just feeding us a bunch of lies." Incredulous, she asked for an example. One of the students said the attack on the World Trade Center was a lie. Dr. Simmons was shocked, dismayed, and motivated. She was going to take these students to Ground Zero. Through connections with *The Daily Show*, there was a successful national fundraising effort. Enough money was raised to take Furr gang leaders, honor students, and chaperones to New York. After the World Trade Center myth was debunked, they toured other sites. While waiting in line to see "42nd Street," one of the students said, "Why are we going to this? I don't want to see a Broadway play!" When the show was over, this same student said, "Can we see another?"

Upon their return to Furr, Dr. Simmons held a faculty meeting. She asked them, "How many of you feel we can turn this school around?" Sadly, almost everyone had a defeatist attitude. Dr. Simmons didn't; she had to clean house. She transferred almost every teacher and brought in a new team of instructors. Then, after a series of meetings, Dr. Simmons and the gang leaders signed a contract guaranteeing peace on the Furr campus. The key component was a commitment to end gang activity at Furr. That contract 15 years later was still in force. Any visitor to Furr discovers a normal though highly active and innovative high school that sends its students on trips to destinations as far as Cambodia and to workshops at many domestic destinations.

In the fall of 2015, Furr began the process of starting a student government by writing bylaws. They began with the model shown above. The evolving product is provided in the Appendices.

There are many ways to skin a cat. At Furr, student empowerment began in 2011 with a "Principal's Court." That's where Dr. Simmons decided to begin. In other places a Principal's Court is called a "Teen Court," "Youth Court," "Judicial Council", "Judicial Board", or the "Supreme Court." Regardless of the name, this is a body that RONR says is made up of people (in this case, students) "recognized for integrity and good judgment." They listen to allegations of impropriety and mete out justice. Justice comes in many academic forms. It's critical to note that at Furr the principles of Restorative Justice (RJ), not suspensions, are in place.

Before Dr. Simmons instituted this program, there were approximately 25 suspensions a day, amounting to a glaring 4500 a year. There have been a declining number of suspensions, and in 2016-2017 there were only two.

RJ requires the offender to make amends to the victim and/or the community. RJ resolves problems and restores relationships. On one occasion, a student pulled the Furr fire alarm; the entire campus had an unscheduled fire drill with associated fire trucks (wasting community resources). Appearing before the Principal's Court, the student only after seeing himself on video, admitted guilt. Punishment was the writing and reading of a multi-page apology. A teacher assisted to be sure the apology was grammatically correct. When it was completed, because the transgression impacted the entire student body, the student was required to read his essay over the school PA system. Most essays are just read to the court. This describes the opportunities for victims and community members to participate in this juvenile justice process. Students do lots of research and because of the give and take with the jurors, they produce amazing projects that show they understand the benefits of the "academic" probation.

A fully functioning Student Government will be the final component of this wonderfully empowered student body that derives this unique power from the school's principal.

A component of RJ at Furr is a room dedicated to conversations where aggrieved parties (usually students) discuss what happened and what can be done to make it right. That room is called "The Thinkery." "I will" statements are used to correct behavior. Beginning on page 6 we referenced the *16 Habits of Mind*. For each student who violates the norm of the school, one habit is selected. If the problem is a failure to Manage Impulsivity, that's what's discussed in depth. There is a follow up if remedial assistance is necessary. If more than two people are involved, community building circles are created. Proverbs abound at Furr. They line the walls and grace many bulletin boards. One that is most apt is the African proverb, "It takes a village to raise a child." That village is definitely in play in implementing RJ.

In "The Thinkery," the student who committed the offense and the person who was offended meet with a mediator. This mediator can be a trained teacher or counselor. The goal is to make things right and the results have been amazing. Students may be required to go to "The Thinkery" as part or all of their "punishment," but administrators of the system report that students are now coming to "The Thinkery" on their own because they are upset and know it works. On other occasions, parents or teachers (or both) are brought in. Often times, the issues are discussed and resolved. Frequently, the problem is a misunderstanding. Sessions can be 15 minutes up to two hours. Follow up is usually not necessary. Sometimes (rarely) things are flip-flopped. Instead of starting in the Principal's Court, the matter is sent to "The Thinkery," where that body gives peer to peer reaction.

It has been reported that sometimes, after a first dispute is resolved, students, feeling empowered, talk with each other using social media. In these cases, they are able to resolve their own issues without adult intervention.

"The Thinkery," established in 2015 and serving a student body of 1200, hears 10 to 50 cases a week. This has resulted in a reduction in the number of Principal's Court cases.

Before RJ, the Principal's Court heard about 35 cases a week; now that number has dropped by half.

Students do lots of research and because of the give and take with the jurors, they produce amazing projects that show they understand the benefits of "academic probation." Most essays are read just to the court.

According to Global Youth Justice, an International Nonprofit Corporation founded in 2015, 1,600 communities on four continents are operating a cost-effective way to reduce the incidence and prevent the escalation of juvenile crime. That figure, 1,600 is not a small one but considering the number of schools in the world, it's obvious that peer-to-peer disciplinary measures are just beginning to materialize.

The utilization of RONR in the creation of a student government is a natural fit in this effort to stimulate appropriate behavior. It's all about civic connectedness. The experts overseeing these programs have evidence to prove that RJ reduces youth incarceration rates. A likely byproduct will be the reduction of adult crime and incarceration.

Now, let's focus on the fine points of disciplinary procedures in RONR. If your school has bylaws that say RONR is your Parliamentary Authority, part and parcel of that is *Chapter XX: Disciplinary Procedures.* For those who are found guilty, obviously RJ penalties are what makes sense. RONR covers everything that can happen in and out of the academic arena. Chapter XX addresses:

1. Offenses in a meeting
2. Offenses outside of a meeting
3. Offenses by members
4. Offenses by non-members

There is specificity in RONR, but here is a general overview.

When an offense is committed by a member of the body in a board meeting, general membership meeting, or any meeting where the people present are officers, RONR can be implemented immediately. The steps are incremental. First the member is given a soft warning by the Chair to return to order. If this warning does not resolve the problem and things either continue or escalate, it's best if a member of the body raises a point of order. It is the responsibility of the Chair to rule on this point. If the response is, "your point is well taken," hopefully this will resolve the problem. If not, the Chair should inform the secretary that they should write down the offending words. If the member persists, the Chair should proceed to a trial. Since the offense occurred in the presence of everyone in the room, only a brief trial is necessary. The accused is given an opportunity to defend themselves. Then a vote is taken. In business meetings to have a (secret) ballot, when a motion is brought before the body, a majority vote is required. In disciplinary cases, though, any member other than the accused can demand a ballot. Expulsion from the meeting requires a majority vote; expulsion from the body requires a 2/3 vote.

When offenses occur outside a meeting, the aforementioned selection of an investigative committee can be done in two ways: 1) by a secret vote of the body, or, 2) by the body assigning this power to the Chair. No member of the body is above the law. If the person under suspicion is the Chair, they must abstain from selecting the investigative body.

RONR is quite dismissive about their own chapter on Disciplinary Procedures. They say, "Ordinary societies seldom have occasion to discipline members." Nancy Sylvester, the author of *The Complete Idiots Guide to Robert's Rules of Order* apparently did not think of their use in schools. She doesn't mention their existence. The same is true in *Roberta's Rules Order*. We included it. RONR, though dismissive of the likeliness of its use, goes to great lengths when it does address discipline. Actually, RONR goes to great lengths to address just about every issue.

Throughout this guide we've tried to provide you with a roadmap on how to create a student government for schools that enroll students in elementary, middle and high school from kindergarten to the 12th grade. Currently, with site based management in vogue, schools are a different "kettle of fish" when it comes to how disciplinary issues will be addressed. The evidence, as a result of reading academic publications and making many personal visits to campuses where facets of what we are recommending is in play, makes us confident that the entire RRAK package, including the disciplinary and restorative approaches described in this chapter, is exactly what's needed to produce a rich and stimulating academic environment. Most importantly schools will produce a much more skillful and engaged citizenry that produces a fair and peaceful world.

"A problem is a chance to do your best."
– Duke Ellington

"We aim above the mark to hit the mark."
– Ralph Waldo Emerson

CHAPTER 5: NUTS AND BOLTS

This chapter covers definitions, principles, and details of what students need to know. Adjust the content to the interests and competency level of your students. A few of these items will likely never be used in school but older students will be knowledgeable of terms and be able to seek additional information as needed. Students participating in competitive events will want to pursue the finer points such as "reconsider and enter on the minutes" or "move the previous question on all pending motions."

VOTING. Let's start with something that at least conceptually seems simple, voting. Voting is necessary to make a formal, definitive decision. Main Motions require a majority vote. A majority is any amount more than half. Some motions, such as the one to limit debate, require a two-thirds vote. The reason Robert's gives for a two-thirds vote is to protect the rights of the minority to have their views heard.

Bylaws should make clear who has a right to vote. Voting is simple and determining the outcome should be as well. Assuming there is little doubt as to who is eligible to vote, *e.g.*, on the Student Council, counting votes should be without rancor. To make sure the voting process goes smoothly, the Chairperson must make sure the members are clear as to what they are voting on.

Students/members often simply say "aye" or "no" in a voice vote. ("Noes" usually shout louder than "ayes.") But if the vote sounds close, then in a small setting a show of hands is needed. If more clarity is needed, the president/presiding officer directs members to stand and, if necessary, be counted. Counting may be by the presiding officer, by tellers, or by counting off. There are several types of voting:

Voice Vote	**Proxy Voting**	**Plurality**	**Roll Call**
Show of Hands	**Bullet Voting**	**Counted Vote**	
Standing Vote	**Written Ballot**	**Secret Ballot**	
Preferential Ballot	**Cumulative Voting**	**Electronic Voting**	

Only when bylaws permit it, such as in homeowners or condominium associations, is ***proxy voting*** permitted. This involves a legal document allowing transfer of one's right to vote to another. One person may collect multiple proxies. It is not a common practice because it is counter to the RONR principle of "one person, one vote." On the other hand, it permits "a voice" for persons who cannot attend a meeting because of schedule conflicts.

Bullet voting occurs when a person has the right to vote for perhaps five members of a committee but only casts one of the five votes and in essence "throws away" the other votes in order to give an edge to a particular candidate.

Many tournaments use a ***preferential ballot*** that enables the judge/evaluator to rank the competitors (usually 1st, 2nd, 3rd and all others 4). If there are multiple judges, the scores are totaled (often in a tabulation room) and the lowest score wins. The next lowest is second and so on. This can be very useful for avoiding deadlocks or time-consuming repeated balloting.

Plurality means getting the most votes but not a majority. This often happens when there are multiple candidates for an office. However, plurality does NOT elect unless the bylaws specifically permit it. This should be determined by the needs of the group. Multiple ballots for large, highly contested elections can be time-consuming, expensive, and potentially disabling for the organization.

Cumulative voting is a somewhat complicated voting method that permits voters to mark several preferred candidates. Votes are then divided among preferred candidates. *Wikipedia* has an in-depth description.

In large elections, it's usual to have a teller's committee that is responsible for counting the ballots and reporting results to the assembly. In highly contested elections, representatives for each candidate should be present as "poll watchers." We have included an example of such a report. It should be signed by the Chief Teller. At the direction of the presiding officer, it is read to the assembly and then read *again* for clarity by the presiding officer who declares the final results such as the candidates elected, the bylaw amendments approved, and so on.

Written ballots are usually **secret ballots** (unless you hand your open ballot to someone else). They should be folded once (not like a piece of origami) and placed in the ballot box or handed to a designated teller. You may leave it blank and turn it in if you wish to privately abstain (disenfranchise yourself).

Electronic voting has become popular as technology catches up with the needs of large bodies of voters. In large assemblies, this involves a clicker mechanism that is activated by a technician at the direction of the presiding officer. For new users, a few minutes of assembly time are needed to make sure members know how to properly use them and to understand the instructions that are normally projected on a large screen.

Roll Call. Sometimes it is appropriate for the secretary to take a roll call vote in which the name of the member is called.

GOVERNING DOCUMENTS

All organizations are subject to the federal, state and local laws of the land. For-profit organizations and many not-for-profit groups must be incorporated according to the state where they must have a registered agent. These groups are incorporated according to their tax status with the Internal Revenue Service [IRS]. For example, they may be a 501(c)(3) religious, charitable, or public service nonprofit, (c)(5) recreational/pleasure, (c)(7) fraternal/pleasurable associations, and so on. Most 501(c) organizations are tax exempt from federal income taxes.

The **Articles of Incorporation** are relatively brief and set up the legal parameters for the corporation. They provide the name, registered agent, purpose and directors (at least three) and the general structure of the organization. They are filed with the Secretary of State. The bylaws of the organization are attached. Bylaws were discussed in Chapters 3 and 4. Two samples are in the Appendices. Organizations may have Standing Rules which typically can be changed by a majority vote. These are procedural in nature. In a large bureaucracy, there are likely volumes of these rules–rules for travel, annual evaluations, reporting expenditures, promotions, interviewing applicants, cleaning buildings, checking out corporation property, *etc.*

RANKING PARLIAMENTARY MOTIONS
ALSO SEE RONR AND APPENDIXES, INCLUDED

All motions, 28 in all, have "standard characteristics" (abbreviated in the charts on pages 125-128 in the Appendices.) These indicate whether the motion can interrupt other business, requires a second, is debatable, is amendable, the vote required for adoption, and whether the motion can be reconsidered.

If each motion is introduced as a spelling word, about one per week during the 2nd and 3rd grades, students will have two years to become familiar with them and be prepared to use them in Student Council in the 4th and 5th grades. Emphasize that most of these words are relevant to large meetings; they do not apply to small board or committee meetings where business is more informal.

Privileged Motions

The five RANKED Privileged Motions do not relate to the Main Motion but are important. They are not debatable and can interrupt whatever else is going on.

Fix the time to which to adjourn sets a future time for the group to meet again in contrast to adjourn at a future time which sets a predetermined time for adjournment. A Standing Rule should establish the time and place of regular meetings. If business is not finished during a meeting, this motion allows a meeting to be set prior to the next regular meeting to complete the agenda. This motion takes precedence over a motion to adjourn. At that "adjourned" meeting, the first item of business is the reading of the Minutes of the incomplete meeting. Business then resumes where the incomplete meeting ended. Although this is the highest ranking motion, it cannot be made when another person has the floor. It must be seconded. It can only be amended to address the date, hour, or place of the adjourned meeting. It is not debatable. A majority vote is required and it can be reconsidered.

Adjourn ends the meeting immediately. A motion to Adjourn is the second highest ranked motion. It cannot be made while another person has the floor. Adjourn means to end the meeting. If the body has approved the agenda and set a time to adjourn but still has business pending, a motion to adjourn must be considered. Once the agenda is approved, a motion to change the time to adjourn requires a two-thirds vote. Certain matters need to be completed before a vote is taken on a motion to adjourn. If there are important announcements, if you need to determine the time for the next meeting, or if the body needs to conclude debate on a motion to reconsider, adjournment is not permitted. A second is required to put the motion to adjourn before the body. With no approved agenda, the motion to adjourn only requires a majority vote. **Adjourn sine die (without a day/time):** Groups in their final meeting adjourn sine die–without a time to meet again. Conventions adjourn sine die because the same group has no designated time to meet again. At some graduations, senior classes adjourn sine die.

Recess: A recess is a break, usually for a short amount of time in the meeting. This motion can be for an immediate recess or for a time in the future. Either the body, the person making the motion, or the Chair can determine the length of the recess. A motion to take a Recess can't interrupt a speaker, must be seconded, is not debatable if business is pending, is amendable, and requires a majority vote. This motion may not be reconsidered. For a very short recess, RONR provides the Chair with the option of telling the body to **Stand at Ease**. This tool allows the Chair, for instance, to consult the Parliamentarian. While this is in force, members remain seated and can talk quietly with their neighbors. Otherwise, talking with neighbors is out of order.

Raise a Question of Privilege: If an individual or body needs to have the Chair address a problem immediately (perhaps to adjust the room temperature or microphone volume), any member can get an immediate ruling by using the Question of Privilege motion. No second and no vote are necessary. For example, if there is noise outside disrupting the meeting, the windows can be closed, but if authority to do so is in question, one can make a request of the Chair: "I rise to a question of privilege affecting the assembly." If someone must leave for a personal matter, he or she says, "I rise to a question of personal privilege." Once recognized by the Chair, the person expresses the concern to get a ruling from the Chair. If the person disagrees with the Chair's ruling an Appeal from the Decision of the Chair can be raised (see Incidental Motions).

Call for the Orders of the Day: This is a request/demand to get back to/stick to the agenda. [A nice way of saying we're off on a tangent and need to get back on track.] The "orders of the day" is the agenda.

Subsidiary Motions

The seven RANKED Subsidiary Motions relate to and must be addressed before consideration of the Main Motion. They are listed here from highest to lowest rank. In other words, Lay on the Table would supersede Postpone Indefinitely.

Lay on the Table (Postpone Temporarily)**:** Allows a majority of the assembly to temporarily set aside the motion under consideration to do something *more urgent*. A tabled motion can be taken from the table after the pressing matter has been concluded. The tabled motion can also be reintroduced as a motion at the next meeting. Tabling delays discussion about a motion. Its purpose is to interrupt the pending business to permit moving to some pressing matter. To table something, say: "I move the question be laid on the table." RONR says this motion is often "incorrectly used." People use it in an attempt to defeat a motion. If the motion to table passes, it takes a majority vote to take the tabled motion from the table. Tabling requires a second; it is not debatable or amendable.

Previous Question (to close debate; vote immediately): The motion, "I move the Previous Question" is used to end debate on the issue at hand. Another way to say it is: "I move that we close debate." Both are correct. A person wishing to make the motion cannot interrupt the speaker who has the floor, but can speak before anyone else wishing to address the body. The motion silences all subsequent speakers if the motion passes. The motion requires a second, is not debatable, is not amendable, requires two-thirds vote, and conditionally can be reconsidered.

Limit or Extend Limits of Debate (may change the number of speakers; but usually changes the time for a particular debatable motion or on all motions): Limit or Extend is used to lengthen or shorten the time or number of times people can speak to a motion. For example, one might say, "I move we allow each person the right to speak three times and for five minutes each time." This motion requires a second, is not debatable, is amendable and can be reconsidered. It requires a two-thirds vote to pass. This "modify the length of debate" motion is not debatable, because *Robert's Rules* suggests it is not logical to debate how many times a person can debate.

Postpone to a Certain Time (same as Postpone Definitely): This motion defers consideration of the motion until another specific time. This motion states that the Main Motion will be addressed at a certain specified time. If there is good reason to take up a subject at a later time, a move to postpone definitely (such as, until 8 p.m. or until a particular person arrives) is appropriate. This motion to Postpone Definitely requires a second, is debatable, amendable and can be reconsidered. It requires a majority vote. The debate must be limited to the merits of the postponement.

Refer to a Committee: If one person feels the motion and/or amendments are taking up too much time or more information is needed, they can move to Refer the Matter to a Committee. This can be an existing committee or a special committee with or without the power to carry out what was decided. A motion to Commit or Recommit (i.e., to send the matter to a committee) requires a second, is debatable and is amendable. Debate is restricted to which committee it should be sent and what powers the committee has. The Motion to Commit or Recommit requires a second, a majority vote, and can be reconsidered.

Amend (primary and/or secondary amendments): This motion changes the wording in the amendable motion to which it applies. Words may be added, struck out, or deleted and inserted. An amendment has to be relevant or related to the Main Motion. "I move to amend the motion by removing the word *baseballs* and replacing it with the word *softballs*," is in an example of a proper amendment. Amendments are debatable and can be amended one time. When an Amendment is amended, this is called a Secondary Amendment or an Amendment to the Amendment. Both Primary and Secondary Amendments require a majority vote and can be reconsidered.

Postpone Indefinitely: If someone presents a Main Motion that a member believes is contrary to the objectives of the organization, postponing indefinitely is the way to get rid of it without actually voting on the motion. It is rarely used. This motion requires a second, is debatable, is not amendable, and requires a majority vote. Only a "yes" vote can be reconsidered. The effect of this motion is to "deep six" it (bury it), or send it to "outer space." The time to bring the motion up again is *never*. The motion is used primarily to kill the Main Motion. It does, however, open the Main Motion for discussion which can be useful if debate is very restrictive or has been exhausted on the Main Motion.

Main Motion

Main Motion: This motion has the lowest rank of the 13 ranked motions and is how new proposals/new items of business are introduced before the assembly. The maker of the motion, after being recognized by the presiding officer/Chair, says: "I move to ... [declarative statement of desired action] ... Such a motion may also take the form of a **Resolution.** In this case, "whereas" clauses stating the reasons for adopting the motion precede the declarative action statement.

Main Motions should be written down before they are introduced. The person making the motion reads it aloud. If it is seconded, it is then given to the Chair. The Chair re-reads the motion to the body. The person who made the motion has the option to speak first. Every member is given two opportunities to speak (debate) for 10 minutes unless there is a contrary Special Rule on the time allowed. Once debate has concluded, the Chair reads the motion for a third time. Then people vote. After the outcome of voting is announced (and if it's obvious no count is necessary), the Main Motion should be given to the Secretary so the exact wording of the motion can be included in the minutes. The outcome of the vote is included in the minutes; the debate is not. The Chair has the authority to require that a motion be written before consideration. This is to insure clarity and helps the secretary as well as the Chair.

To avoid confusion, students need to understand that ranking motions are disposed of in reverse order from the way they are originally introduced.

Each of these motions must be seconded and then restated by the chair. It may be required by the chair or the secretary that they are submitted in writing.

For example:

Speaker **one** moves that a bear be adopted as the school mascot.

Speaker **two** moves to strike "bear" and insert "wildcat."

Speaker **three** moves to strike "wildcat" and insert "cougar."

Speaker **four** moves to refer the matter to a committee of five.

Speaker **five** moves to amend five and insert "three appointed by the Chair."

Speaker **six** moves to close debate and vote immediately on all pending motions. [*aka "move the previous question on all pending motions."*] **Vote. Motion carries.**

What happens next? What does the Presiding Officer do?

Without further debate, the Presiding Officer puts each question to a vote and announces the result starting with the last motion (an amendment) in this manner:

"Debate is closed on all motions before the assembly. The pending motion is to "strike five" and insert "three appointed by the Chair." Those in favor say 'aye.' [pause; count if needed] Those opposed say 'no'. [pause; count if needed] The noes have it; the amendment is defeated. The question now before the assembly is whether to refer . . .to a committee of five. [take vote in same manner; motion fails].

Chair: *"The motion to refer to a committee failed. Now before the assembly is the secondary amendment to amend the amendment by striking wildcat and inserting cougar." Vote. Motion carries.*

The motion before the assembly is the primary amendment to strike "bear" and insert "cougar." Vote. Motion carries.

Chair: *"The assembly is now voting on the Main Motion as amended which reads that the school mascot be a cougar." Vote. Motion carries.*

Chair: *"The assembly has adopted the Main Motion as amended and we will now recognize the cougar as the new school mascot."*

* * * * *

Incidental Motions (No rank; listed alphabetically)

There are 11 Incidental Motions. Incidental Motions are related to the Main Motion. The use of one comes into play based on a set of circumstances related to the Main Motion. They must be decided immediately, even before the ranking motions: Subsidiary and Privileged (described earlier), such as the ones related to adjournment. Most Incidental Motions are decided by the Chair and are not debatable. The best way to understand them is by looking at the circumstances in which they occur.

Appeal from a Decision of the Chair: Used when one believes the Chair/presiding officer has made an incorrect ruling. If the Chair/presiding officer does not change their ruling and the appeal receives a second, debate ensues. The Chair may speak first or second and last. Everyone else can speak only once. After debate is finished, the assembly is asked to vote to sustain (aye) or overturn (no) the opinion of the Chair. A majority or tie "aye" vote sustains the decision of the Chair.

Close Nominations and Polls: A speaker may move that the polls be open or that they be closed. A speaker may also move that nominations cease or be re-opened. There are several possibilities. RONR provides for a variety of ways to nominate officers. The bylaws address this issue of nominating and ending voting in an election in two ways. RONR is silent on the issue of campaigning, speech making and other aspects of an election. This is consistent with the way things work in American politics. The opportunity for voters to hear the views of the candidates is haphazard, whether it's for President, Mayor, City Council or other elected offices. Initially, the most important thing to be done is to fill in the blanks in your bylaws related to time and frequency of elections. As things evolve, it may be necessary to refine your bylaws to cover more of the election process. It can also be done by creating Special Rules.

Committee of the Whole: When a member feels adequate information is available from the people present, but more needs to be said right now, the Committee of the Whole, Quasi Committee of the Whole or Informal Discussion can be used. Utilizing any of these tools gives more time to discuss the matter than the normal limits of debate: two times and ten minutes. These three motions require a second, are debatable, are amendable, and require a majority vote. Once discussion starts, these matters cannot be reconsidered. This permits open discussion without motions, and can be useful when a group is uncertain about a course of action and is not pressed for time.

Consider by Paragraph or Seriatim:. The recommended approach when adopting bylaws or any other lengthy document for any organization is to consider them *seriatim*, which means by paragraph. Each paragraph is debated independently. This means people have two opportunities to debate the document. Someone must move to Consider Seriatim if the Chair fails to suggest it. This motion requires a second. It is not debatable but is amendable. It requires a majority vote and may not be reconsidered. After a review of each paragraph, and after voting on amendments to each paragraph (if applicable), the entire document is placed before the body for amendments, debate and a final vote.

Division of the Assembly: If the Chair does not automatically do this, a member can request a counted vote. If a voter questions the accuracy of a vote, especially a voice vote, he or she may call for a Division of the Assembly. If the objector wants a counted vote and the Chair does not feel this is necessary, if the Chair feels the request is dilatory (a waste of time) because the outcome of the vote was obvious, the request can be denied. If someone still wants "a division" they must make a motion and get a second. This motion is not debatable. A majority vote in favor of a motion to have a different type of vote is required to force taking time to conduct the counted vote. Many times, *RONR* presents a conundrum for the Chair: Is a Call for a Division of the Assembly a vote that can be a counted vote? This must be decided by the Chair and illustrates why it is important to have a fair and impartial Chairperson. When faced with highly contentious or important votes, the Chair has the choice of skipping voice and hand votes, and using a standing or counted vote. One way to do this is for people to sit in identical seating arrangements on opposite sides of the room (hence the term "Division of the Assembly") or some other accurate division to determine the will of the body. Some votes require a two-thirds majority vote to determine the outcome. Two-thirds (in the majority) votes are not voice votes. An example would be a vote to Move the Previous Question (close debate and vote immediately). The Chair does not need to count votes when a vote's outcome is obvious. A quick survey of the room is sufficient. If the Chair is in doubt, a count should be taken. The quickest way to determine if a two-thirds majority has been achieved is to double the "no" votes. If these "noes" exceed the "yes" votes, a two-thirds majority was not achieved.

Examples:

If the vote to close the debate was:

> 6 "YES" votes
>
> 4 "NO" votes x 2 = 8
>
> 6 is less than 8,

there is **not** a two-thirds majority and debate continues.

If the vote had been:

> 7 "YES" votes
>
> 3 "NO" votes x 2 = 6
>
> 7 is greater than 6,

so a two-thirds majority **was** achieved. The motion to close the debate carries and debate ends.

Dishonest counting is a way to disrupt or even kill an organization. A manipulated vote is clearly a way to win in an underhanded way. Such problems can happen in many meetings including a Student Council meeting. RONR is designed to minimize the chances of this happening.

Division of the Question: This is used to separate a complex motion into parts. It's wise to have separate votes on a long motion. This allows certain parts to pass without accepting parts that are objectionable. This is often used when the majority of the body supports one part of the motion and wants to get that part passed even if other parts are rejected. An example of this would be when two library books are under consideration. One part of the motion is to buy one book, and it passes while another part of the motion to buy another book is rejected. It makes sense to Divide the Question so that selecting one book doesn't cause the rejection of both books. Regarding this process, RONR says "little formality is involved… It is arranged by unanimous consent." This requires no second, no debate and no vote.

Objection to the Consideration of a Question: This motion is used when someone opposes the Main Motion for a highly principled reason. Before debate begins, he or she can say, "I object to the Consideration of the Question." The way this motion is presented by the Chair is: "There is an objection to the motion to … All those in favor of considering…say 'aye.' All those who oppose consideration of the motion, say 'no.'" If there is not two-thirds present and voting who oppose the motion, it will be considered (debated and approved or rejected). This motion can interrupt a speaker, it does not need a second, and it is not debatable or amendable.

Parliamentary Inquiry: Used to request information about parliamentary procedure such as whether the making of a motion would be in order or what vote is required to adopt a motion.

Point of Order: This motion calls attention to a breach in rules. It is the job of the Chair to make sure that the rules are followed. It is the job of the members to follow the rules. To restore order when things get chaotic, a Point of Order demonstrates meeting etiquette and may be the most significant motion RONR has available. Examples include when members are speaking without raising their hand to be recognized and when two or more people are talking at the same time. When people are truly committed to the goals of the organization and appreciate the need for proper decorum, this rule may be used less. If people behave improperly, members may use a Point of Order. While some rules seem tricky, a Point of Order is easy to make although the person (or people) for whom the Point is raised may take offense. When a member feels things are out of order and the Chair hasn't called the offender out of order, the member can interrupt whatever is happening to say, "Point of Order." No second is required. The Chair stops everything and has the person who called for a Point of Order to "state your point." If the Chair agrees, he or she will say. "I sustain your Point of Order. Will the member please come to order?" If the Chair is unsure, he or she can ask members to vote on the Point of Order. If a majority agrees, the Point of Order is sustained and those who are out of order are called to order. Except for a brief explanation of what the Point of Order is for, it is not debatable or amendable.

Request for Information: This provides the opportunity for a member to ask a question of the Chair (such as what is the proper motion that a member should use to accomplish a goal) or, through the Chair, to ask the treasurer whether there is enough money in the budget for such a purchase. This is a simple request. It is not for an exposition on a matter.

Suspend the Rules: If it's a Special Rule, this motion requires a 2/3 vote. If it's a Standing Rule, it requires a majority vote. If passed it has the effect of temporarily negating a rule. These rules have restrictions; except for rules in RONR, they usually cannot be suspended.

Voting/Elections: There are many motions relating to voting and elections such as when to open or close the polls or others that affect the procedure for conducting an election. See RONR for details.

Withdraw a Motion: A request from the maker of a motion who would like permission from the assembly to withdraw a motion after it has been seconded and thus becomes the province of the body. This motion requires a second if made by the maker of the motion, is not debatable, and requires a majority vote.

Bring Back Motions/ Restoratory Motions

(Bringing a motion back before the assembly can be complicated. For precise details, see RONR.)

Amend Something Previously Adopted: This motion is used to change the wording in a motion previously adopted that has not been executed. The same rules that apply to rescind a motion apply here; you may modify a motion and not defeat it completely.

Discharge a Committee: Terminates a committee that has completed its work or has failed to adequately perform its assigned responsibilities.

Reconsideration: Reconsideration is used when someone on the prevailing side changes his or her mind about a motion after the vote has been announced. The person seconding the motion does not have to be from the "prevailing" side. If the matter to be reconsidered is debatable, so is the motion to reconsider. It is not amendable. It requires a majority vote and cannot be reconsidered. This matter of reconsideration might also be called the "go home vote." If something passed, such as a Main Motion, it can be reconsidered. Don't leave a meeting after something passes unless you are sure the decision will stand. Someone may move to reconsider. Reconsideration is a way you can reverse something during a meeting. If you have received new information and you wish to change your vote you can say, "I move to reconsider the action relative to [whatever is to be looked at again, such as the purchase of books for the library].

Rescind: Negates a motion that was passed at a previous meeting. It undoes something previously adopted that any member feels was incorrect. To make this motion one says, "I move that we rescind [whatever the action was]." This debatable motion must be seconded. To pass it requires a majority vote if it was on the agenda. If no notice was given, passage requires a two-thirds vote. It is too late to rescind an action if the action [whatever the action was, *i.e.*, purchase of a new book for the library] has already taken place. If you have passed a budget but only part of the funds have been spent, you can "move to rescind or amend [whatever unspent portion of the budget you wish to reallocate]."

Take from the Table (resume consideration): This motion is used to bring back a motion that was temporarily set aside. It requires a second, is debatable, is not amendable, requires a majority vote, and can't be reconsidered.

Rules of Debate

This is an arena of wide flexibility. If no Special Rules have been adopted for an assembly, RONR allows each member the opportunity to speak two times for a maximum of ten minutes each time. This proves excessive for many groups with limited meeting time, long agendas or very vocal members. Any group can adopt Special Rules (by 2/3 vote) to define how debate shall be conducted as to length of time per speaker, total time allotted to a subject, number of speakers on given topic, and so forth. These may be adopted and codified for all discussions, for a convention, or for situations until officially changed. Committee rules regarding debate must be established by the assembly; committees may not establish their own rules unless they have been authorized to do so by a higher authority such as in the bylaws, Standing Rules, or instructions from the assembly.

Keep your sense of humor.

A light approach to some matters may serve you well.

The force of public opinion cannot be resisted when permitted freely to be expressed. Whenever the people are well informed, they can be trusted with their own government.
— THOMAS JEFFERSON

CHART I: Ranking Motions with Standard Characteristics

	MOTION	May interrupt when another has the floor	Requires a second	Debatable	Amendable	Vote Required for Adoption	Can it be reconsidered
Privileged Motions	Fix Time to Which to Adjourn	No	Yes	No	Yes	Majority	Yes
	Adjourn	No	Yes	No	No	Majority	No
	Recess (include length of time)	No	Yes	No	Yes	Majority	No
	Raise a Question of Privilege	Yes	No	No	No	None Chair handles	No
	Call for Orders of the Day (agenda)	Yes	No	No	No	Chair handles	No
Subsidiary Motions	Lay on the Table/Postpone Temporarily	No	Yes	No	No	Majority	Negative Only
	Previous Question/Move to Close Debate	No	Yes	No	No	Two-thirds	Yes
	Limit or Extend Limits of Debate	No	Yes	No	Yes	Two-thirds	Yes
	Postpone to Certain Time	No	Yes	Yes	Yes	Majority	Yes
	Commit or Refer to a Committee	No	Yes	Yes	Yes	Majority	Yes
	Amend	No	Yes	Yes***	Yes	Majority	Yes
	Postpone Indefinitely	No	Yes	Yes	No	Majority	Yes*
	Main Motion	No	Yes**	Yes	Yes	Majority	Yes

Note: Motions on this chart are listed in order of "rank," beginning with Main Motion, which is lowest. When a motion is amendable but not debatable, any amendments to such motion are undebatable. Call for the Orders of the Day and Question of Privilege require no vote—only action by the Chair.
* Affirmative vote only.
** A motion made by a committee of two or more members does not require a second.
***If applied to a debatable motion.

CHART II: Common Incidental Motions with Standard Characteristics

INCIDENTAL MOTIONS (not ranked)	In order when another has the floor	Requires a second	Debatable	Amendable	Vote Required for Adoption	Can be reconsidered
Point of Order	Yes	No	No	No	None	No
Appeal	Yes	Yes	Yes	No	Majority[1]	Yes
Suspend the Rules	No	Yes	No	No	Two-thirds	No
Objection to Consideration	Yes	No	No	No	2/3 in neg.	Neg. vote only
Division of a Question	No	Yes	No	Yes	Majority	No
Consideration by Paragraph	No	Yes	No	Yes	Majority	No
Division of the Assembly	Yes	No	No	No	None[2]	No
Motions relating to voting and nominations	No	Yes	No	Yes	Majority[3]	Yes[4]
Requests and Inquiries	Yes	No	No[5]	No[5]	Chair handles	No
Request for a Privilege	Yes	No	No	No	Majority	No

1. Majority or tie vote sustains the decision of the Chair
2. On the demand of a single member, the Chair must take a rising vote
3. Except motion to close polls or affirmative vote on motion to reopen polls
4/5. Except Request to be Excused from a duty

CHART III: Restoratory Motions (Bring Back) with Standard Characteristics

Restoratory (or Bring Back Motions)	In order when another has the floor	Requires a second	Debatable	Amendable	Vote Required for Adoption	Can be reconsidered
Take from the Table	No	Yes	No	No	Majority	No
Reconsider (at same meeting)	No[1]	Yes	Yes[2]	No	Majority	No
Rescind (at a subsequent meeting)	No	Yes	Yes	Yes	Two-thirds[3]	Negative vote only
Amend Something Previously Adopted	No	Yes	Yes	Yes	Two-thirds[3]	Negative vote only
Discharge a Committee	No	Yes	Yes	Yes	Two-thirds[4]	Negative vote only

1. The making of the motion is in order when another has the floor, but before the speaker begins.
2. Is debatable ONLY if the motion to be reconsidered is debatable
3. Or majority if previous notice is given, or majority of the entire membership.
4. Or majority if previous notice is given.

GLOSSARY: Parliamentary Terms

Accept–To adopt or approve a motion, or a report. See Adopt.

Adjourn–A motion to end a meeting.

Adopt–A vote to accept a motion or a report.

Agenda–A detailed and specific list containing items of business to be brought forward at the meeting.

Amendment–A motion which modifies the wording or meaning of a pending motion.

Assembly–The members of an organization who have met for the purpose of transacting business.

Bylaws/Constitution–The fundamental rules (laws) governing the affairs of a society, and defining the duties and privileges of its members and officers. The bylaws supersede any of the rules of its parliamentary authority with which they are in conflict. Sometimes a constitution has a higher amending threshold.

Chair–This term refers to the person in a meeting who is presiding at the time, whether that person is the regular presiding officer or not. The same term applies to the presiding officer's station in the hall from which he or she presides, which should not be permitted to be used by other members as a place from which to make reports or speak in debate during a meeting. Chairman; the presiding officer, regardless of official title.

Consensus–General Consent/Unanimous Consent: A form of voting in which no objection is voiced.

Convention–A delegate body in a usually large meeting or series of meetings usually developed around a particular theme or common purpose. In conventions of elected delegates, three key committees which must report at the first session are the **Credentials**, **Rules** and **Program Committees**.

Cumulative Voting–A multiple-winner voting system intended to promote more proportional representation than winner-take-all elections.

Executive Session–All or part of a meeting that is closed to the public; only certain individuals may attend. (Also see Closed Session.)

Ex-officio–"By virtue of office". Sometimes without a vote. This person is not counted as part of the quorum.

Germane–Closely related (*e.g.*, amendments must be *germane* to the Main Motion).

Illegal Ballot–A ballot cast for an ineligible candidate or one that is unintelligible.

Incidental–These motions "pop up" as the situation dictates; the highest priority incidental motion is a "point of order." An example of "low" priority is a request to read papers.

Keynote/Guest Speaker(s)–One or more specialized speakers who present a talk at a general session. Often these are notable individuals who draw attention and participants to the meeting. Prepared remarks of introduction are typically made by the president or program chairman.

Lectern–Reading desk with slanted top.

Main Motion–Introduces business before the assembly.

Majority Vote–More than half of the votes cast.

Meeting–Single gathering of members in one room or area to transact business.

Minutes–The record of actions taken by the organization; sensitive matters may require initials of the secretary and president on each page for verification; such records must be kept in a permanent file; digital backup notwithstanding. Often a copy is kept in the President's book as well as the Secretary's.

Motion–A formal proposal in a meeting that brings business before the assembly or calls for a ruling by the Chair. There are five categories of motions: Main, Subsidiary, Privileged, Incidental and, Bring Back. See the three charts of motions on page 59-62 or 125-128.

NO MOME CPA–This is the mnemonic for the Articles in a basic set of bylaws; namely, Name, Object (or Purpose), Membership, Officers, Meetings, Executive Committee, Committees, Parliamentary Authority, and Amendments.

Obtaining the Floor–The process of receiving formal recognition from the presiding officer for speaking or offering a motion. To do this the member rises and addresses the Chair by official title, then waits until the Chair recognizes the member by name, title, or some other sign. Sometimes a member may interrupt the proceedings; at other times one waits to be recognized.

Order of Business–An established procedure or plan which prescribes the chronological order in which different classes of subjects or business shall be considered.

Parliamentary Authority—The manual of parliamentary law and procedure which an organization has adopted to use in the conduct of its business, for instance Robert's Rules of Order Newly Revised (RONR).

Pending—A question is "pending" once it has been stated by the Chair and until it has been disposed of. Should several questions be pending before the assembly at the same time, the last one stated by the Chair is called the immediately pending question because it will be the first one to be acted on.

Plurality Vote—Getting the most votes but not a majority; the largest number of votes received when there are three or more choices.

Precedence—Has priority over or ranks above.

Preferential Voting—Rank ordering one's preferences on a ballot when permitted to vote for more than one person. It is used by many tournaments because it enables the judge/evaluator to rank order the candidates (usually 1st, 2nd, 3rd and so on). If there are multiple judges, the scores are totaled (often in a tabulation room) and the recipient with the lowest score is the winner or is elected. The next lowest is second and so on. This can be useful for avoiding deadlocks or time-consuming repeated balloting.

Privileged Motions—The five highest ranking motions. They have a rank within themselves.

Previous Question—A motion to stop debate and to proceed to voting.

Primary Amendment—An amendment of the first degree; that is applied to the Main Motion.

Pro Tem—For the time being, temporarily.

Proxy Voting—A written authorization that permits another person to cast one's vote/ballot.

Quorum—The number of members that must be present for the legal transaction of business. Robert's recommends that when establishing this number, you do so after determining how many people are likely to normally attend a meeting, discounting days when there is inclement weather. This number or percentage should be in your bylaws.

Recess—A short intermission in the proceedings.

Reports—Summaries of activities of committees or officers. These may be written, oral, or a combination of both. Printed reports that contain information only are filed with the secretary. Reports that have action items–recommendations, *etc.*, require a majority affirmative vote for adoption. Such issues should be placed on the agenda in advance of the meeting.

Resolution–A form of Main Motion usually of such length, formality, and/or complexity that it should be precisely worded and submitted in written form.

Script–Prepared remarks for handling motions with cues for use by the presiding officer and others which can indicate agenda, names of guests, accurate language to be used in introductions and debate.

Second–An indication by a second member of a desire to have the proposed motion discussed.

Secret Ballot–Written ballots by which one's vote is not revealed to others.

Session–A single meeting or a series of connected meetings (as in a convention) devoted to a single order of business, program, agenda, or announced purpose.

Special (Ad Hoc) Committees–Special committees are created by the assembly for a specific task; usually short-lived; especially in comparison to standing committees which exist until removed from the bylaws or voted out of existence.

Special Meeting–A meeting called for a specific purpose.

Special Rules are rules adopted by an organization that supersede the governing instrument, likely RONR. They may be adopted or amended by a 2/3 vote or a majority of the entire membership. Such rules may specify the order of business, agenda format, length and number of times members may speak on a given topic, or whether motions may only be submitted in writing. They are often found after the (but not part of) the bylaws. They may be part of a separate Procedures Handbook.

Standing Committees–These are the committees listed in the bylaws. The bylaws indicate their membership (how they are constituted), powers, terms of office, and so on.

Standing Rules are "housekeeping rules." They may address dates, starting time, place of meetings, duties of committee chairmen, arrangement of rooms and more. Standing Rules are adopted or changed by majority vote. Standing Rules are often found in a Procedures Handbook separate from the Bylaws and Special Rules.

Subsidiary Motions–Seven motions that apply to the Main Motion; such motions have an important priority among themselves.

Two-thirds vote—Two-thirds of the votes cast. This vote is never a voice vote. A hand vote is the simplest way to conduct this vote. If, in the opinion of the Chair, the outcome is in doubt, time should be devoted to a counted vote.

Viva Voce Vote or Voice Vote—This is a vote taken by voice.

Written Ballot—This is a vote taken with a marked paper ballot.

Bonus Words:

The following are words that exist in other governing instruments but do not appear in RONR.

Bullet voting occurs when a person has the right to vote for perhaps five members of a committee being elected but only casts one of the five votes and "throws away" the other votes to give an edge to a particular candidate.

Closed Session—A meeting that is available only to those with tickets or special invitations usually obtained before the meeting begins. Boards and committees may also vote to go into "Executive Session." These meetings and proceedings remain private.

Conference theme—A special themed focus which may be for a short-term meeting around which general sessions, or a series of short sessions, or combined with the term of office of the president. It will likely involve decorations, logos, banners, special characteristics of meetings, and public relations efforts woven together.

Consent—Agreement.

Dais—A platform raised above the floor of a hall or large room.

Meeting Planner—A person whose primary job responsibilities are the planning and management of the convention or meetings. Such person may be vice president/president-elect or an employee of the organization sponsoring the meeting(s). Professional meeting planners or employees of a convention center may also be used.

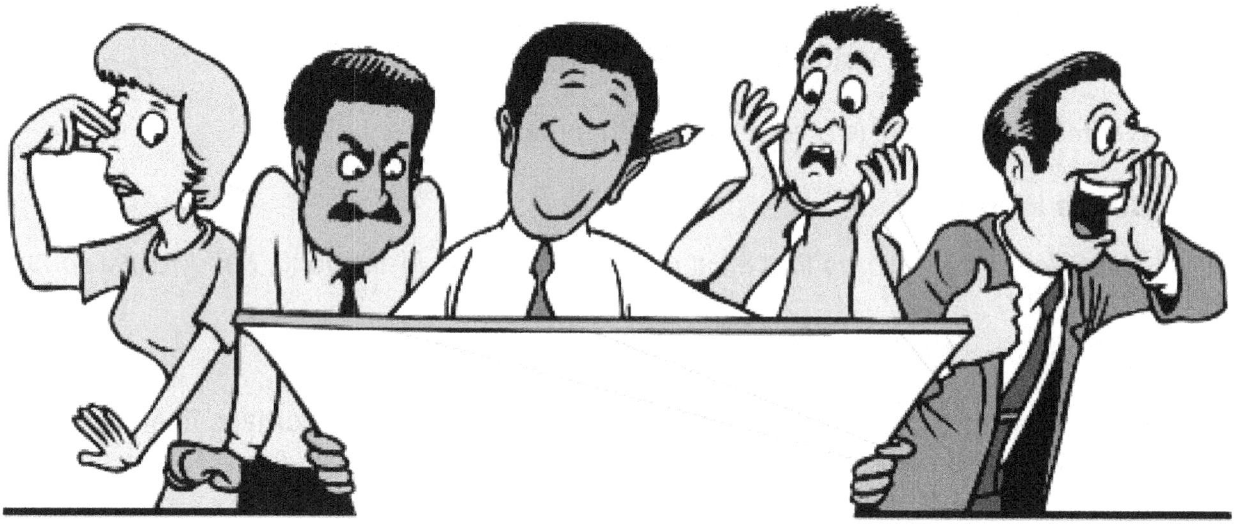

CHAPTER 6: A BRIEF HISTORY OF HENRY MARTYN ROBERT & DEMOCRATIC DECISION-MAKING

A BRIEF HISTORY OF ROBERT'S RULES

In the Preface to the 11th edition of Robert's Rules of Order Newly Revised, there's a fascinating history of not only this seminal work, but also the documents that preceded it.

The authors of that book point out that the original version was published in February 1876, 100 years after the founding of the United States. They describe a 14-hour meeting chaired by U.S. Army Colonel Henry M. Robert in New Bedford, Massachusetts, that thoroughly frustrated him. He said, "It was a disaster...and accomplished almost nothing." The focus of the meeting was how to protect the city from a possible attack by the Confederate Navy. After the meeting, Robert, a member of the U.S. Army Corps of Engineers, vowed never to attend another meeting until he knew something about Parliamentary Law. His research paid some dividends but nothing that completely satisfied him. Subsequently, he wrote 16 pages of parliamentary rules for use in lay assemblies but discovered they were inadequate. Thirteen years later he completed and published the first edition of his guide to conducting better meetings. Today, the 11th edition, published in 2011 is 716 pages plus a Preface to the 11th Edition, an introduction and Principles Underlying Parliamentary Law.

Robert pointed out that, "the holding of assemblies...is doubtless a custom older than history." He brings history alive as he spells out the various customs that evolved.

Shortly after the publication of the new and enlarged 11th edition by Sarah Corbin Robert, Henry M. Robert III, William J. Evans, Daniel H. Honemann, and Thomas J. Balch, Robert's 90+ year-old grandson, Henry M. Robert III, came to Texas to celebrate its publication. He visited the Galveston Seawall to see, near Ft. Crockett Seawall Park, a plaque for the first time that commemorates the work of his grandfather. Robert's grandson was being honored for his grandfather directing the building of the seawall following the Great Galveston Hurricane of 1900, where an estimated 6,000 to 12,000 people were killed.

In 1915, another hurricane of similar strength hit the city with a loss of only 11 lives

In 1915, another hurricane of similar strength hit the city with a loss of only 11 lives in the Galveston town area. This is a graphic testament to the engineering genius of Henry Robert.

Today Henry Robert is better known for *Robert's Rules of Order*. While no one will ever be able to say for certain that his guide to meeting order saved lives, we do know for certain that it has empowered people in ways they never would have imagined.

Henry Robert was born in South Carolina. His father moved the family to Ohio because of his strong opposition to slavery. Robert's grandson told the annual convention of the Texas Association of Parliamentarians in 2011 that his great-grandfather (Robert's father), Joseph Thomas Robert, was the first President of the Augusta Institute, later renamed the Atlanta Baptist Seminary, then the Atlanta Baptist College. Today it is known as Morehouse College. Morehouse is the alma mater of the Reverend Dr. Martin Luther King, Jr.

Robert's grandson told the convention that after the 2nd edition of *Robert's Rules* was published (and this does not appear in the 11th edition or any other edition of the book), Robert went to his father and asked him if it could be reviewed by what are now called "the Men of Morehouse." That review led to the addition of 26 pages of text and the 1893 third edition.

In 2012, we called Morehouse to find out how much influence *Robert's Rules* had in the education of Dr. King. The representative of the Martin Luther King International Chapel said he had had the same question. He said that Robert's grandson had recently been there and they were trying to find out when *Robert's Rules* ceased being a significant part of the curriculum. They were considering its reintroduction.

The principles in this book have roots in the British Parliament and the writings of Thomas Jefferson as well as the *Rules of Order* by Henry M. Robert contained in *Robert's Rules of Order Newly Revised*.

The preface to *Robert's Rules of Order Newly Revised (RONR)* includes 12 fascinating pages about how Henry Martyn Robert, U. S. Army Brigadier General and a leader in the Baptist church, became interested in conducting productive meetings and how his work has evolved. Robert was an amazing man who made major contributions to this country in a variety of ways. We recommend that you purchase a copy of his book, RONR, to read not only about him but also to learn about the development of democratic decision-making. *Robert's Rules of Order in Brief*, another option, is a good starting point and may be purchased through the National Association of Parliamentarians on their website www.parliamentarians.org.

DEMOCRATIC DECISION-MAKING

Governeur Morris, a largely unknown name in American history, wrote The Preamble to the U.S. Constitution:

We the people of the United States, in order to form a more perfect union, establish Justice, insure domestic Tranquility, provide for the common defense, promote the general Welfare and secure the Blessings of liberty to ourselves and our Posterity, do ordain and establish this Constitution for the United States of America.

Morris and many other brilliant minds throughout history have put into writing why "forming a more perfect union" (including organizations) is important.

The Constitution was not meant to be a document for a barren land; it was written for all the people who inhabit it. The preamble should inspire people to establish organizations, whether in schools or communities that will take students from childhood to the end of life, and will help carry out the democratic process. Many contemporary thinkers have also expressed concern at the loss of the democratic process.

Having a clear purpose and using it to chart your course is fundamental to having a successful organization. The authors of the United Nations charter, signed in 1945 when the world was recovering from World War II, must have been inspired by the Preamble to the U.S. Constitution when they wrote these words:

We the peoples of the United Nations determined

- *to save succeeding generations from the scourge of war, which twice in our lifetime has brought untold sorrow to mankind, and*
- *to reaffirm faith in fundamental human rights, in the dignity and worth of the human person, in the equal rights of men and women and of nations large and small, and*
- *to establish conditions under which justice and respect for the obligations arising from treaties and other sources of international law can be maintained, and*
- *TO PROMOTE SOCIAL PROGRESS AND BETTER STANDARDS OF LIFE IN LARGER FREEDOM,*

And for these ends

- *to practice tolerance and live together in peace with one another as good neighbors, and*
- *to unite our strength to maintain international peace and security, and*

- *to ensure, by the acceptance of principles and the institution of methods, that armed force shall not be used, save in the common interest, and*
- *to employ international machinery for the promotion of the economic and social advancement of all peoples,*

Have resolved to combine our efforts to accomplish these aims.

Accordingly, our respective Governments, through representatives assembled in the city of San Francisco, who have exhibited their full powers found to be in good and due form, have agreed to the present Charter of the United Nations and do hereby establish an international organization to be known as the United Nations.

Who can dispute the desire expressed here? But the more fundamental question is: do the member nations practice what they preach?

The United Nations (UN) has a set of sophisticated rules for the implementation of this charter.

When organizations are not true to their stated principles, their future is bleak. But with commitment and clear rules of procedure, people can move mountains.

CHAPTER 7: SCRIPTING, SAMPLE SCRIPT

Scripting is a useful tool for learning and for assuring accuracy. A script includes a set of prepared remarks with cues for use by the presiding officer and others which may indicate the agenda, names of guests, announcements, *etc.* as well as accurate language to be used in introductions and/or in presenting business. Speakers receive copies of the script in advance and rehearse it until they know the script thoroughly; so well that they know their parts, with possible options depending on motions made, and it is not obvious that they are reading. They are to maintain eye contact with the audience and keep speaking in a normal voice.

We learn by acquiring information (reading, observing different roles), through direct experience, by role-playing and by modeling (imitating the behavior of another person whom we admire). How does one become an excellent secretary or presiding officer? Study the requirements (job description is usually in the bylaws or standing rules/procedures manual/RONR). Mentally rehearse and visualize yourself in the role. Then try it — preferably starting in a small organization with a minimal work load.

Scripts may also be scenarios for learning by role-playing. One such script is included in this chapter.

Using Scripts

Role-playing by using well-prepared scripts serves several purposes:

1. It models to students how scripts may be prepared to better manage meetings. Used frequently, the language becomes familiar and, by playing different roles, students learn the various technicalities in the scenario.
2. By preparing a script for the presiding officer for a large and/or important meeting, it can reduce the psychological stress on the presiding officer and contribute to a smoothly run meeting.

Parliamentary Law Drill on the Precedence of Motions

This demonstrates how all the Subsidiary and Privileged Motions and selected Incidental Motions may be employed, and left pending, while a single Main Motion is before the Assembly. The original drill, by Mrs. Leone C. Newby, was written for 53 members. It was revised to serve 12 members of a ladies' club in 1950 by Mildred Steele Rupley and published in the *National Parliamentarian.* In that case the Chair remains seated for most of the meeting because the group was functioning as a committee. In a large meeting with the president on a dais, the president will stand most of the time but not when members are expressing their opinions on the Main Motion unless by sitting his or her view of the people in the hall would be obstructed. The characters for this board meeting, as differentiated from a small board meeting of 12 or less, were modified, the script reformatted, and expanded to include 14 board members by Martha Haun in spring 2016.

***　　　***　　　***

OFFICERS:

President	ALICIA
Secretary	CAYDEN
Treasurer	CHARLIE
Parliamentarian	MARTHA

BIG BAYOU KIDS KLUB BOARD MEMBERS

JACKSON	STEPHEN	MARK	EMILY
BOBBY	MISSY	GEORGE	PEGGY
TED	LOUISE		

[The meeting was properly called to order and a quorum established. It has progressed through the normal order of business and is now returning from a recess. It will begin by addressing New Business.]

President ALICIA: The meeting will come back to order. Order means silence except for the chair or a recognized speaker talking: one person at a time.

JACKSON: Madam President.

President ALICIA: Jackson.

JACKSON: Since our attention has been called to certain needs of the new neighborhood Recreation House, I move that we donate 50 books to their reading room and install a drinking fountain in their gymnasium.

STEPHEN: I second the motion.

President ALICIA: It is moved and seconded that we donate 50 books to the reading room of the new Recreation House and that we install a drinking fountain in the gymnasium.

GEORGE: Madam President, I object to the consideration of the question. *[This motion does not require a second and is not debatable.]*

President ALICIA: The consideration of the question has been objected to. Will the assembly consider it? Those in favor of considering the question will please rise.

ALL RISE–except PEGGY and GEORGE.

President ALICIA: "1, 2, 3, 4, 5, 6, 7, 8. Eight in the affirmative. Be seated. Those opposed will please rise. PEGGY and GEORGE both rise.

President ALICIA: 1, 2. Two in the negative. There being less than two-thirds in the negative, the objection is not sustained and the question will be considered.

[Note: RONR does not require a counted vote; the presiding officer must, of course, personally be clear that there are 2/3 in the affirmative and has the option of audibly counting.]

MISSY: Madame President. I rise to a parliamentary inquiry.

President ALICIA: The member will state her inquiry.

MISSY: Is not a single member's objection sufficient to prevent the consideration of a question?

President ALICIA: Will the Parliamentarian please answer the member's question?

Parliamentarian Martha: An objection to the Consideration of a Question is one of the Incidental Motions that requires a two-thirds vote in the negative, on the motion to consider the question, to sustain it. In the case of obtaining general consent or, as it also called "a unanimous vote" for any proposed action, one member objecting defeats it. These two points are often confused.

STEPHEN: There surely can be no greater need than food for the mind which our gift of books would represent, and pure drinking water for one's health. It seems to me this would be one of the most important needs we could care for. Absolutely, I favor the resolution as presented.

President ALICIA: Stephen, you were not recognized by the Chair and however well-meaning your comments may be, they are out of order. Are you ready for the question?

EMILY: Madam President.

President ALICIA: Emily.

EMILY: I move that the question be postponed indefinitely.

MISSY: I second the motion.

President ALICIA: It is moved and seconded to postpone the question indefinitely. Are you ready for the question?

BOBBY: Madam President.

President ALICIA: (assigning Bobby the floor with a nod).

BOBBY: As has been brought out in debate of the Main Motion, there is a possibility of other demands of greater urgency being brought before the club later; therefore, I feel it would be well to postpone this question indefinitely.

MARK: Madam President.

President ALICIA: MARK.

MARK: I think it would be a very great mistake to indefinitely postpone this question, as in the letter they write, they speak of the necessity of knowing just what they will be able to depend upon. This is particularly true of the drinking fountain as the gymnasium is not yet completed and it would, doubtless, save considerable expense and trouble to install the fountain before the work is finished. And, as a matter of economy for our own club, it certainly would be to our advantage to buy any books we should contemplate buying at the present time as the Nameless Book Store is offering a very attractive discount on all classifications of books until the close of this month. The discounts range from 25-40%, and they are willing to further cooperate in the matter of gift books in large numbers by contributing an additional number to the order. I have one of their folders here that I should be glad to read if I may.

President ALICIA: If there is no objection, MARK will be allowed to read a paper bearing on the subject of debate. Is there any objection?

GEORGE: Madam President, I object.

MARK sits down.

STEPHEN: Madam President, I move that permission be granted to MARK to read the paper in connection with his speech on the question.

President ALICIA: The question is on granting MARK permission to read his paper.

EMILY: Madam President, I rise to a point of order.

President ALICIA: The member will please state her point.

EMILY: There was no second to the motion.

President ALICIA: The point is not well taken. Will the parliamentarian please give the basic principles of seconds to motions.

Parliamentarian MARTHA: Madam President, the basic principle of seconds to motions is that the assembly shall not be required to consider any question–except a very few specially listed motions–to which at least two members do not agree to bringing before the assembly. In the present case, the member having asked permission to read a paper, and another member having moved that such leave be granted is an agreement of two to submitting the question to the assembly; therefore, it is the equivalent to a motion and a second.

PEGGY: I rise to request information.

President ALICIA: The member will please make her request.

PEGGY: I should like to know if it is not the duty of the parliamentarian to watch all points of parliamentary procedure and to correct us when we make mistakes; such as not seconding motions when they require a second, and so forth–and to see that the members do the right thing generally.

President ALICIA: It is a common error for clubs to regard the Parliamentarian as something like a policeman, but her office does not include law enforcement. It is the DUTY of the president to enforce the rules of the assembly and is the privilege of any member to require that she adhere to the duties of her office when any infraction of a rule occurs. Hence, it would be unjust for the president to try to evade an unpleasant duty by attempting to place it on the parliamentarian, and presumption on the part of the parliamentarian to try to assume the prerogative of the executive officer. The question is on the adoption of the motion to grant leave to Mrs. Brand to read a paper as part of her speech. Those in favor say AYE.

STEPHEN and MARK: AYE.

President ALICIA: Those opposed say NO.

ALL OTHERS: NO.

President ALICIA: The NOES have it and permission to read papers is refused. Stephen, do you wish to speak further in debate of the question?

STEPHEN: No, Madame President, I have concluded my remarks.

President ALICIA: The question before the assembly is on the motion to postpone the question indefinitely. Are you ready for the question?

TED: Madam President.

President ALICIA: TED.

TED: I move to amend the motion by striking out "50" before "books" and inserting "100."

MARK: I second the amendment.

President ALICIA: It is moved and seconded to amend by striking out "50" before "books" and inserting "100" which, if adopted, would make the resolution read that we donate 100 books instead of 50. Are you ready for the amendment?

STEPHEN: Madam President.

President ALICIA: Stephen.

STEPHEN: I am very much in favor of the amendment as presented, since we have this opportunity to express the civic sense of the club, I think we should do it in a big way.

EMILY: Madam President.

President ALICIA: Emily.

EMILY: I do not favor the amendment as I feel that 50 books would adequately express our civil sense–also such a gift would be more consistent with the amount of money we have in the treasury.

MARK: Madam President.

President ALICIA: Mark.

MARK: I move to amend the amendment by adding "by modern writers."

GEORGE: I second the motion.

President ALICIA: It is moved and seconded to amend the amendment by adding "by modern writers." Are you ready for the amendment to the amendment?

BOBBY: Madam President, I rise to a point of order.

President ALICIA: The member will please state the point.

BOBBY: I do not consider the amendment to the amendment germane.

President ALICIA: The member raises the point of order that the amendment to the amendment just offered is not germane. The Chair is in doubt and submits the question to the Assembly. As many as are of the opinion that the amendment to the amendment is germane, say '"Aye."

ALL (except BOBBY): AYE.

President ALICIA: As many as are of the contrary opinion say, "NO."

BOBBY: NO.

President ALICIA: The "Ayes" have it and the assembly considers the amendment to the amendment germane. The question is on the adoption of the amendment to the amendment by adding "by modern writers." Is there further debate on the amendment to the amendment?

MARK: Madam President?

President ALICIA: Mark.

MARK: Since those spending most of the time at the recreation house are mainly the younger set, I am of the opinion that they would enjoy books by modern writers more than those by earlier writers.

MISSY: Madam President.

President ALICIA: Missy.

MISSY: The objection to buying books by modern writers is that it takes time to prove their worth so we might, in such a collection, get a large number of books that would not live–and so be of little value with the passing of time.

President ALICIA: The question is on the adoption of the amendment to the amendment by adding "by modern writers," which would make the amendment read: "100 books by modern writers." Are you ready for the amendment to the amendment?

PEGGY: Madam President.

President ALICIA: Peggy.

PEGGY (IMPROPER): I move to amend the amendment to the amendment to the amendment by inserting the words: "best of the" before "modern writer."

President ALICIA: Additional amendments are out of order as there can only be an amendment and an amendment to the amendment.

BOBBY: Madame President.

President ALICIA: Bobby.

BOBBY: I move to refer this matter to a committee to be appointed by the president.

TED: I second the motion.

President ALICIA: It has been moved and seconded to refer this matter to a committee to be appointed by the president. Is there discussion?

JACKSON: Madame President.

President ALICIA: Jackson.

JACKSON: I think this is a matter that should be taken care of with the least possible delay since those in charge of equipping the recreation house would like to know what to depend on; I do not favor committing the question.

President ALICIA: Is there a speaker in favor of the motion to refer this matter to a committee?

BOBBY: Madame President.

President ALICIA: Bobby.

BOBBY: I am very much in favor of referring this matter to a committee, and to obviate the delay mentioned by the member who has just had the floor, we could have an adjourned meeting and ask that the committee report to it.

President ALICIA: Are you ready for the question?

GEORGE: I move to postpone the question to the next meeting.

BOBBY: I second the motion.

President ALICIA: It is moved and seconded to postpone the question to the next meeting.

Peggy: (IMPROPER)–Madam President, I have no patience with this whole procedure. There is too much red tape to it. Why doesn't the president TELL us what she wants us to do, and we will go ahead and do it without all this bother.

President ALICIA (rising with gavel in hand which she lightly brings down on the desk): This is a democratic organization and, as such, it is the duty of the President to first ascertain the will of the assembly and then to impartially enforce the rules and resolutions it adopts. We will proceed with the deliberation of the assembly. Are you ready for the question on the motion to postpone to the next meeting?

TED: Madam President.

President ALICIA: Ted.

TED: I agree with the point that has already been made: The best interests of the Recreation Center would be served by not delaying the vote on this question. Therefore, I do not favor the motion to postpone the question to the next meeting.

STEPHEN: Madam President.

President ALICIA: Stephen.

STEPHEN: I think this is a matter concerning which we should not reach a hasty conclusion, and, in my opinion, it will either have to be very thoroughly discussed in this meeting or else be postponed in order to have time to consider it later and, since our time may be somewhat limited today, I favor postponing it to the next meeting.

President ALICIA: Are you ready for the question?

LOUISE: Madam President.

President ALICIA: Louise.

LOUISE: I move that debate on the immediately pending question be limited to four minutes.

MISSY: I second the motion.

President ALICIA: It is moved and seconded to limit debate to four minutes. Are you ready for the question?

JACKSON: Madam President.

President ALICIA: Jackson.

JACKSON: I move to amend by striking out "four" before minutes and inserting "eight."

STEPHEN: I second the motion.

President ALICIA: It is moved and seconded to amend by striking out "four" before "minutes" and inserting "eight." Are you ready for the question? …SILENCE…

President ALICIA: Those in favor of the amendment to strike "four" and insert "eight" say AYE.

JACKSON: AYE.

STEPHEN: AYE.

President ALICIA: Those opposed say NO.

ALL OTHERS: NO.

President ALICIA: The NOES have it and the amendment is lost. The question is on the motion as originally stated: to limit debate on the immediately pending question to four minutes. Are you ready for the question?

EMILY: Madam President.

President ALICIA: EMILY.

EMILY: I move the previous question on the immediately pending motion to limit debate to four minutes and on the motion to postpone the question to the next meeting.

BOBBY: I second the motion.

President ALICIA: The previous question is moved and seconded on the immediately pending motion to limit debate to four minutes and on the motion to postpone the question to the next meeting.

PEGGY: Madam President, I called for the question myself.

President ALICIA: Order please. An individual member calling for the question has no power to cut off debate. Only a two-thirds vote has the power to do that. The question is on the adoption of the previous question. Those in favor will rise.

President ALICIA: 1, 2, 3, 4, 5, 6, 7, 8…Eight in the affirmative. Those opposed rise. MISSY and GEORGE rise. 1—2—Two in the negative. Two-thirds favoring the ordering of the previous question.

President ALICIA: We will come to a vote on the motion to refer to committee the resolution which is as follows: "that we donate 50 books to the reading room of the new recreation house and that we install a drinking fountain in the gymnasium and all pending amendments. Those in favor say AYE. All vote Aye except MISSY, GEORGE, and EMILY.

President ALICIA: Those opposed say "NO." MISSY, GEORGE and EMILY vote NO.

President ALICIA: The Ayes have it and the resolution is adopted and the motion that the club donate 50 books to the reading room of Recreation House and install a drinking fountain in the gymnasium is referred to committee. What is the further pleasure of the assembly?

MARK: Madame President.

President ALICIA: Mark.

MARK: I move to adjourn.

EMILY: I second the motion.

President ALICIA: There are a number of important details to be attended to in connection with appointment of a committee to carry out the order just adopted; but since we are to have an adjourned meeting closely following this one, those matters can be attended to later. The question, therefore, is upon adjournment. Those in favor say AYE.

ALL: Aye.

President ALICIA: Those opposed say NO. (silence). The ayes have it and the meeting stands adjourned to Tuesday night at 7 o'clock.

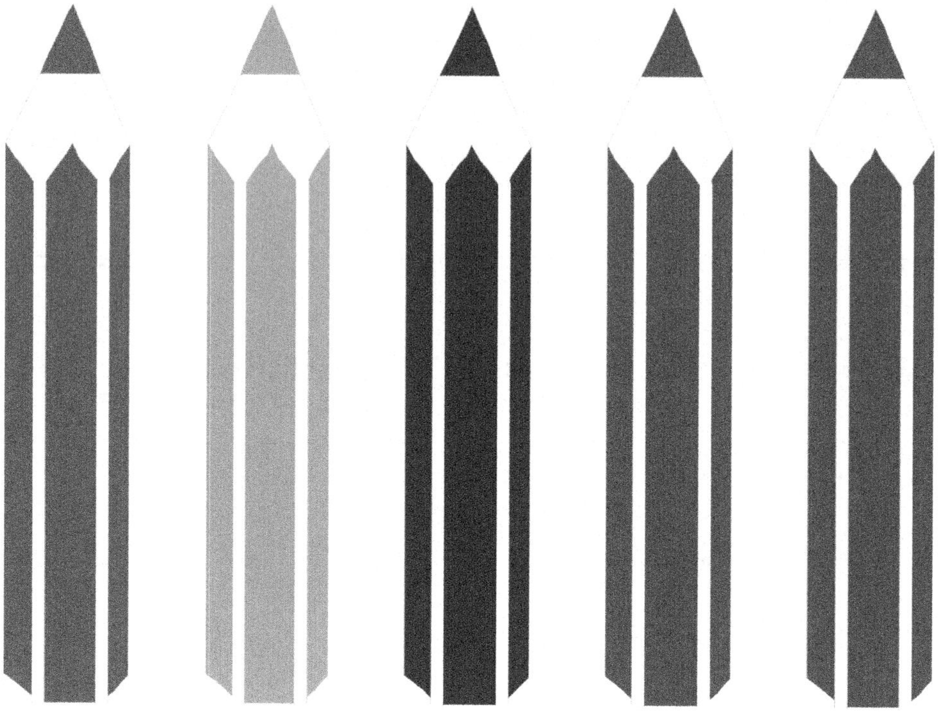

CHAPTER 8: MEET THE AUTHORS:

Martha's Story

Martha Womack Haun, Ph.D., PRP, is accredited by the National Association of Parliamentarians as a Professional Registered Parliamentarian and is the editor of the *National Parliamentarian* (NAP). Dr. Haun is a member of the American Institute of Parliamentarians and was editor of the international *Parliamentary Journal* for seven years. She has authored or co-authored more than two dozen articles on the parliamentary process and won national recognition for her co-authored work with Dr. Robin Nicklin Williamson at the University of St. Thomas [Houston], "Let the Minority Be Heard." She has also published in the *Free Speech Yearbook* [on Spinoza and free speech], and on Immanuel Velikovsky [vs. establishment science] published by the National Communication Association. Dr. Velikovsky is the author of *Worlds in Collision.* Dr. Haun has taught parliamentary procedure/effective meeting management and other communication classes at the University of Houston for more than 45 years and has done hundreds of workshops and seminars at local, state, and national levels.

Dr. Haun has always been determined to model those causes she believes in. For several years in the 70s she Chaired the Women's Caucus of the National Speech Communication Association. She coached debate teams at Stetson University in Florida and at the University of Houston (UH) while giving birth to three daughters in four years during the semester breaks. At UH she was Chair of the Academic and Professional Women's Council.

She has long been an advocate for hearing the minority voice (see citations for Spinoza and Velikovsky articles). She received the AIP President's Award for her co-authored article on minority rights. She has taught at the university level for more than 50 years, helping students find voice through student government, debate, and in interpersonal crises. Specific venues for the latter include Lifeline Chaplaincy Board of Directors for 18 years [Houston], Fuller Family Life Therapy Board [Houston], Rolling Futures Board [Dallas], and local, state, and national parliamentary organizations.

Three times she has Chaired the National Commission on American Parliamentary Practice [CAPP] and received their Distinguished Service Award. In 1999, she was named Educator of the Year by the Texas Speech Communication Association. For several years she coached nationally award-winning HOSA [Health Occupation Student Association] teams at DeBakey High School for Health Occupations, Houston, Texas.

Dr. Haun is Past National President, Professional Fraternity Association, and was an officer or board member for five years. PFA represents more than one million Greeks in professions nationwide. She is a Past National President, Phi Beta National Professional Fraternity for Creative and Performing Arts, and has been a national board member for more than 15 years. She served two terms as National President and many years as their National Parliamentarian. She is parliamentarian to a variety of national, state and local professional groups and Houston area homeowners associations.

She has received over $100,000 in personal and team curriculum development grants since 2000. Besides effective meeting management, Dr. Haun also teaches communication theory, health communication and crisis communication across the lifespan.

In 2016, she was unanimously elected as First Vice President/President-elect of the Texas State Association of Parliamentarians. She served many years as parliamentarian to the University of Houston Faculty Senate and Undergraduate Council and has Chaired curriculum and numerous other committees. She is a national parliamentary consultant to a number of national and state organizations including the Academic Language Therapists Association (ALTA), the International Multisensory Structured Language Education Council (IMSLEC) and The ALLIANCE. The latter three groups focus on teaching persons with dyslexia.

Her B.S. in Secondary Education (Speech and English) and Master of Arts (Speech Communication and Educational Psychology) are from the University of Texas at Austin. Her Ph.D. in Rhetoric and Public Address is from the University of Illinois at Champaign/Urbana. She has taught numerous parliamentary workshops for parliamentary programs including S.W.A.T. (Spread the Word Across Texas) for the Texas State Association of Parliamentarians, student government officers and Greek organizations at the University of Houston, as well as parliamentary organizations at the national, state and local levels. Dr. Haun was the recipient of the 1999 University Educator of the year by the Texas Speech Communication Association.

Dr. Haun has written three textbooks including *Communication: Theory and Concepts (2014), Crisis Communication (2014),* and *Effective Meeting Management (2015).*

In spring 2016 she was honored to have the Phi Beta Fraternity endowed scholarship for the Valenti School of Communication at the University of Houston named in her honor. That year she was again elected to a two-year term as National President of Phi Beta National Professional Fraternity for the Creative and Performing Arts.

Articles

Williamson, Robin Nicklin and Haun, Martha Womack (2015). "Redefining an Organization: The Role of the Parliamentarian," *Parliamentary Journal,* January 2015, Vol. LVI, *1* (January 2015). pp. 5-10.

Haun, Martha J. and Williamson, Robin N. (2014). "Impression Management and the Presiding Officer." *Parliamentary Journal*, LV July 2014.

Williamson, Robin Nicklin and Haun, Martha Womack. "Listening Skills for the Parliamentarian, *Parliamentary Journal,* April 2013, Vol. LIV, no. 2, pp. 60-65.

Haun, Martha J. and Williamson, Robin N. (2013). "Rational Authority and the Parliamentarian: Avoiding Power Struggles." October 2013. *Parliamentary Journal, pp.*121-128;

Haun, Martha J. and Williamson, Robin N. (2010). "Creating Positive Organizational Climates through the Culture of Parliamentary Law," *Parliamentary Journal,* October 2010.

Haun, Martha J. and Williamson, Robin N., "Saving Face in Organizations," *Parliamentary Journal,* January 2009, pp 29-34.

Haun, Martha J. and Williamson, Robin N., "Parliamentary Portals; Gateways to Goals," *Parliamentary Journal,* April 2008, pp. 51-58.

Haun, Martha J. and Williamson, Robin N. "From Reactive to Proactive: Avoiding Costly Mistakes." *Parliamentary Journal*, July 2006.

Haun, Martha J., and Williamson, Robin N. "Let the Minority Be Heard." *Parliamentary Journal,* July 2005.

Received 2006 Presidential Award for Excellence in Writing on Parliamentary Law, American Institute of Parliamentarians.

Haun, Martha J., and Williamson, Robin N. "Is There Any Discussion?" *Parliamentary Journal,* October 2000, pp. 153-156.

Haun, Martha J. "What Does Non-Adoption Signify?" *Parliamentary Journal,* October 1998, pp. 158-159, American Institute of Parliamentarians.

Haun, Martha J. "American Parliamentary Debate," *Parliamentary Journal,* July 1998, pp. 102-104.

Haun, Martha J. "The Professional Convention Parliamentarian," *Parliamentary Journal*, July 1987; reprinted in *Readings in Parliamentary Law*, pp. 95-101, American Institute of Parliamentarians, 1992.

Haun, Martha J. "The Role of the Faculty Senate Parliamentarian," *Parliamentary Journal,* July 1991, pp. 86-89. American Institute of Parliamentarians.

Haun, Martha J. and M. Romberg. "Questions of Recognition in a Large Meeting," *Parliamentary Journal*, July 1980; reprinted in *Readings in Parliamentary Law*, pp. 65-72, American Institute of Parliamentarians, 1992.

Haun, Martha J. "The Professional Convention Parliamentarian," *Parliamentary Journal*, July 1987, pp. 82-88. American Institute of Parliamentarians.

Haun, Martha J. and Robin N. Williamson, "A Case for Theoretical Foundations in the Undergraduate Communication Curriculum," *Texas Speech Communication Journal,* May 1985, pp. 39-44.

Haun, Martha J. "Parliamentary Puzzles as a Teaching Methodology," *Parliamentary Journal,* July 1985, pp. 95-99; 113. American Institute of Parliamentarians.

Haun, Martha J. "The Effect of Ex Officio Members on the Quorum of a Small Committee," *Parliamentary Journal*, January 1984, pp. 35-37.

Haun, Martha J. "A Rationale for Using Robert's Rules of Order Newly Revised without Substantive Modification," *Parliamentary Journal, July* 1982.

Haun, Martha J. "Functions and Duties of the President in a Complex Organization," *Parliamentary Journal*, July 1982, pp. 113-118.

Haun, Martha J. "The View from Behind the Gavel: Correct and Effective," *Parliamentary Journal*, October, 1981, pp. 125-126.

Haun, Martha J. "Instructional Models for Handling Substitute Motions," *Parliamentary Journal*, July 1981, pp. 108-110.

Haun, Martha J. & Romberg, M. "Questions of Recognition in a Large Meeting," *Parliamentary Journal*, July 1980, pp. 1-7.

Haun, Martha J. "Immanuel Velikovsky: A Case Study in the Suppression of Scientific Ideas," *Free Speech Yearbook*, Speech Communication Association, 1979, 27-37.

Haun, Martha J. "Parliamentary Perspectives on the International Women's Year Conference: 1977" *Parliamentary Journal*, April 1978, pp. 7-10. American Institute of Parliamentarians.

Haun, Martha J. "Spinoza: On Freedom of Expression," *Free Speech Yearbook*, Speech Communication Association, 1977, pp. 47-53.

Books

[in progress] with Leandra Hernandez, Ph. D. *Crisis Communication in Health Contexts: Process and Practice Across the Lifespan.*

Haun, Martha J. and Weisgal, Ted. *Robert's Rules for Kids and Big Kids: A Guide to Teaching Kids of All Ages the Basics of Parliamentary Procedure, 2016.* Wise Wit Publishing Company, Houston, Texas.

Haun, Martha J. (with D. Clark and R. Williamson) *Managing Meetings Effectively.* McGraw-Hill, 2015.

Haun, Martha J. *Communication: Theory and Concepts*. 7th ed., McGraw-Hill Primis, 2014.

Haun, Martha J. *Crisis Communication: Process and Practice*. 2nd. ed. McGraw-Hill Primis, 2002.

Haun, Martha J. and Quintinilla, Guadalupe. *Estrategias efectivas para hablar en publico.* McGraw-Hill Primis, 2001.

Haun, Martha J. *Public Speaking Workbook*. 3rd ed. McGraw-Hill Primis, 2000.

Haun, Martha J. and Michael L. Fain.*Competitive Oral Interpretation*. McGraw-Hill, 1995.

Haun, Martha J. *Texas Speech Communication Association Leadership Handbook*, 1989.

Chapter

Query, Wright, Amason, Eichhorn, Weathers, Haun, Gilchrist and Klein. "Using Quantitative Methods to Conduct Applied Communication Research." In, Frey, Lawrence R. and Cissna, Kenneth N. *Handbook of Applied Communication Research:* Routledge, 2009.

Areas of Teaching Specialization: Health, Interpersonal, Family, & Crisis Communication; Communication Theory; Meeting Management; Public Address, Argumentation and Debate, Business and Professional Communication. Workshops include nonverbal communication, stress managements and parliamentary procedure.

Curriculum development (courses created that are part of the current curriculum):
COMM 1302: Introduction to Communication Theory
COMM 1333: Interpersonal Communication
COMM 3332: Effective Meeting Management (formerly Parliamentary Procedure)
COMM 4335: Crisis Communication
COMM 6341: Crisis Communication Across the LifeSpan

Grants
$40,000 grant, fall 2006, Medical certification project, Distance Learning with Jim L. Query, Jr. and Larry Kelly, co-principal investigators, and Shawn McCombs.

$25,000 grant, May 2005. Haun, M. Principal Investigator, with Query, Jim L., Jr., development of Center for Health and Crisis Communication, see www.uh.edu/chcc
$6,000 grant, summer 2006, Houston Alzheirmer's Association, Query & Haun, Center for Health and Crisis Communication, website development project.
$7,000 grant, fall 2006, Houston V.A. Hospital, Query & Haun, pain management project, Center for Health and Crisis Communication, audio-visual development project.

Honors
Alpha Delta Kappa, International Honorary Sorority
Phi Beta National Professional Fraternity
Pi Kappa Delta, National Honorary Fraternity

Martha's Acknowledgments

Foremost I thank my co-author Ted Weisgal for sharing this journey with me and persisting until a workable plan emerged. I was in the state convention audience a few years ago that voted to postpone such a project as this indefinitely. Not because it wasn't a good idea but because there was no plan of action, because we know how full the public school curriculum is, and that most subjects have to be cleared by the State of Texas Coordinating Board before there is much chance of reality.

After continued reflection though, I realized the great number of private schools there are (with a more flexible curriculum) and the huge number of home-schooled children there are (five next door to me and two UH charter school students on my cul de sac who inspired parts of the long script and who kindly watch kid shows on my TV to keep me awake when I consider napping instead of typing). There will be brave and creative public and private school teachers and administrators who see the value in what we propose and will find ways beyond what we have suggested to implement these concepts.

I thank my three daughters (Kim Haun Havely in Denver, and Chandra Haun Muenster in Dallas who long ago asked to "borrow that hammer thing" and special thanks to my Houston daughter Charissa Haun-Crump for her assistance in formatting the final copy of this book) for their continued support in whatever I choose to do. I thank the superb parliamentarians who have gone before me to forge a trail, refine the profession and provide the advanced training that has shaped me to whom I am today; for those early mentors and colleagues– John Stackpole, Bill Southworth, Hy Farwell, William Tacey and others; for friends like Ann Guiberson, PRP, Mary Randolph, PRP, CPP-T, Kay Alison Crews, PRP, CP-T, Kirk Overby, PRP, Richard Hayes, PRP, Dennis Clark, PRP, Lucy Anderson, JD, PRP, Jonathon Jacobs, PRP, CP, my long-time (not old) Houston communication colleague and parliamentary co-author at University of St. Thomas, Robin Nicklin Williamson, Ph.D., as well as numerous other members and staff of the Texas State Association of Parliamentarians, the National Association of Parliamentarians and the American Institute of Parliamentarians. A special thanks goes to C.J. Ransom, PhD, plasma physicist, for his encouragement and manuscript review and endorsement, and for his long-time friendship that has roots in our hometown, Denison, TX, and in our mutual interest in giving voice to the works of Dr. Immanuel Velikovsky.

I am honored to have served for two terms as 1st Vice President of the Texas Association of Parliamentarians and editor of the *National Parliamentarian*, a professional trust I do not take lightly! Thanks to my colleagues in the Valenti School of Communication who love and support their senior faculty! Special thanks to "D" and "Z" who have made the Martha Womack Haun Phi Beta Fraternity Endowed Scholarship in Communication at the University of Houston a reality! I'm proud to be part of the University of Houston faculty!

Peace and blessings to you all,
Martha Womack Haun, Ph. D., PRP

Ted's Story

While we were in the midst of writing this book, we heard a critique by the hosts of the MSNBC show, "Morning Joe." They were critical of the Democratic Party in Wyoming saying that although Bernie Sanders, a candidate for President of the United States, received a substantial majority of the votes, it appeared he was getting a minority of the delegates. A guest tried to explain that this was happening because of "the rules." We won't get into the minutia of Democratic Party rules. We just want to use this example to underscore the importance of rules.

Robert's Rules of Order Newly Revised (RONR) is the universal standard for democratic decision making. We hope you will develop an appreciation for its history dating back to 1876 and take note of the fact that it has been revised and improved multiple times. Its 11th edition was published in 2011.

The one event that really got me interested in the democratic process was a 1962 college student government meeting. But the seed was planted much earlier. Born in the shadow of the movie industry in Hollywood, California, I was an only child until the age 10 and quite lonely. My parents were from New York City. My closest relatives lived in Chicago. The natural way most people connected through family didn't apply to me.

As a union organizer, my father attended many meetings. Because union rules excluded outside visitors, I never attended one with him. My mother attended many meetings, too, including the League of Women Voters. Both of my parents supported Civil Rights, Women's Rights, and, as stated in the Preamble to the U.S. Constitution, "the general welfare."

Throughout my high school years, I participated in a journalism program sponsored by the Hearst newspaper in Los Angles, the Scholastic Sports Association. During my senior year, in 1962, I served as Editor and had the privilege of writing columns. One (see Appendix F) addressed the question, why isn't there interscholastic sports for girls? Ten years later, the federal government passed Title 9. When I, assisted by my editor, Dave Kirby, wrote the column, I felt that it was only a matter of time. The rush I got from seeing that column in print whetted my appetite for being an advocate for positive social change. It's taken a long time to get from there to here but that experience played a significant role in motivating me to write this book.

As a freshman journalism student at Los Angeles Valley College I attended a meeting of the student government. My best friend, Stan Taylor, had done the same thing and came away appalled at the chaos and lack of productivity. I, on the other hand, observed something foreign and fascinating: their attempt to utilize *Robert's Rules of Order*. Among the things that I observed was the Student Government president wrongly declaring that abstentions went to the majority. It seemed wrong at the time but I had no knowledge of the book and, for years, did not question it. I spent many years in different organizations passing this error on to others. [I wonder how many people are still repeating this misinformation.] Perhaps my guilty conscience played a role in writing *Robert's Rules for Kids* and this expanded effort, *Robert's Rules for Kids & Big Kids*.

My first leadership position in college was as president of the B'nai B'rith Hillel chapter. Hillel is a social organization for Jewish students. Before becoming the president, I was in charge of the publicity for events and fundraisers. Hillel's membership quickly jumped from 12 to over 100. The members thought my efforts were a key to this growth. At this time, the Civil Rights Movement was dominating the news and with the increasing popularity of folk music and protest songs, I tried to get the B'nai B'rith to provide financial backing for a concert and fundraiser featuring many popular folk acts that were performing in the area. We had most of the details worked out with the Ash Grove, a popular nightclub in L. A., but we couldn't convince B'nai B'rith that we had the marketing skills to make the event a success. This led to my deciding Hillel was not the right fit for me.

A couple of friends and I decided to start a new campus organization, *Friends of the Student Non-Violent Coordinating Committee*. SNCC was a national organization about to launch Mississippi Freedom Summer, a massive African-American voter registration drive and alternative school program. We drafted bylaws and took them to the Dean of Students. He told us we couldn't receive recognition if we affiliated with a national organization. I asked, "What about Circle K and their relationship with Kiwanis?" His response: "That's different." Deciding that it wasn't worth a fight, we named ourselves the *Student Civil Rights Organization (SCRO)*. There was another barrier to climb. We had to receive InterClub Council approval to become an official campus organization. After receiving that recognition, about 60 people attended our first two meetings. At the second meeting, someone nominated me for president. I declined saying, "No, we need to have an African-American." I received spontaneous applause for the first time in my life. I realize now that this was both unfair and racist since the only known qualification would be race. The consequence was that SCRO shriveled up and died.

A short time later, I was elected Vice President of the Sophomore Class. We really didn't have identifiable constituents. Nevertheless, the Sophomore Class President and I decided to organize a campus-wide book drive with donations going to Mississippi Freedom Summer. We raised over 10,000 books. A box company donated the boxes we needed to ship the books to Mississippi. I wanted to go too but my parents said no. Three students, James Earl Chaney, Andrew Goodman and Michael Schwerner, were killed by the Ku Klux Klan. It might have been me.

By this point, the die was cast; I loved being an activist. I loved taking an idea from conception to fruition.

The success of a book-drive reaped rewards. I was asked to join The Knights, a Men's Honor Service Organization. This group served the college at major events. I was asked to usher at a speech by Madame Nhu, the First Lady of Vietnam. In the fall of 1964, I had never heard of Vietnam. I arrived late. I was shocked to see the 1200 seat facility filled with people of my parents' generation. I thought Mrs. Nhu was nuts when she announced the sons of the people in the audience would be fighting in her country in the very near future. When I got home, my parents explained that Vietnam, formerly French Indochina, had been fighting a war for many years. There have been many gaps in my education. Knowledge about RONR was one; understanding Southeast Asia was another.

As secretary of The Knights, I carried out my duties all wrong. Oblivious to the fact that RONR had clear instructions on what belongs in minutes and what doesn't, I took copious notes at each meeting. At the subsequent meetings, I read my notes which caused numerous disputes over the content. Many years later, I discovered that I was not supposed to write down what people said but what we were going to do.

One student government leader, Mitch Robinson, decided to start a club with the sole purpose of having fun. He wrote bylaws and Scaboritus was born. Robinson's mother loved weekend parties. Based on my experience with SCRO, I doubted that the members of the InterClub Council would recognize the club, but membership was quickly approved and I became a charter member. Friendships counted.

The following semester, I entered San Jose State and in the spring was elected President of my dorm. I began my campaign by making individual 8 ½" by 11" sized letters that spelled out the phrase, "Red Ted 4 Dorm Head." I hung the letters on the dorm stairwell. My opponent (or his friends) rearranged the letters. I asked my roommate, Jim Bailey, what I should do. He told me to let it go. People seemed to be more interested in me as a result of the games my opponent played. The advice Bailey gave me not only paved the way to my winning the dorm leadership position but having it on my resume helped me get a job with Volunteers in Service to America (VISTA), a part of the federal government's War on Poverty.

The turmoil the 60s is known for what was starting to bubble. Reflecting on 1966, three things stand out for me.

The first was arranging for Professor Robin Brooks to lecture on the history of Vietnam. Unfortunately, we didn't test the waters to determine if in our dorm there was interest in the subject. Thus, attendance was sparse. Had we used *Robert's Rules*, we might have approached this event more methodically assessing interest first and then organizing publicity accordingly.

The second was the flooding of Allen Hall. That semester only five of the six wings were occupied. A student decided to stop up all the drains in the empty wing and turn on the showers. Water ran into every room on the floor below. At 6 a.m. the dorm mother was frantically calling me on the PA system to come to her office. I already knew something was up and wanted no part of the disciplinary process.

In situations like this, *Robert's Rules* calls for the formation of a committee to do an investigation. If the evidence justifies a trial and penalties, the entire organization gets involved. Since I didn't know *Robert's Rules*, I thought the entire burden for disciplining this student would fall on me. I disappeared for a week. This did not endear me to the dorm mother and my term ended on a flat note.

The third experience was at an Inter-Club Council meeting. I introduced a motion to make one of the dorms co-ed. The motion was soundly defeated. Had I known *Robert's Rules* better, I would have introduced a motion to set up a committee to study the issue to make it more palatable. Two years later, when I finished my stint with VISTA and returned to San Jose State, there was a high-rise co-ed dorm accommodating over 650 students.

It's not easy being a rebel but it does have its advantages. In 1966, VISTA was a new organization. I went through a six-week training program at the University of Maryland School of Social Work in Baltimore. Trainees came from all over the U.S. Some of the "seasoned" members were on the training staff. One night we collected money to purchase records to play in the dining room. I joined the committee and suggested we buy *If You Can Believe Your Eyes and Ears* by the Mamas and Papas. A seasoned vet objected. Since there was no mechanism like *Robert's Rules* to settle the dispute, I bought the record myself. It became the most popular album at the training center.

My VISTA assignment was at Baltimore's Garrison Junior High. Getting there required two buses. My job was to use my "amazing persuasive powers" to get dropouts back to school. The first student was a 13-year old developmentally delayed African-American girl. She dropped out the previous year after she had a very bad stomach ache that turned out to be a baby. When I got to her apartment, I heard from the other side of the door, "Be quiet. The truant officer is here." No matter how much I tried, the door never opened. My second effort was no better. A young boy was a recent transplant from Appalachia. His father told me his son complained that he was required to shower and change clothes with black students (he used a less genteel word) and that they harassed him. The father said he was just waiting until his son turned 16 when it would be legal for the boy to drop out of school.

After these two experiences, I told the principal that the project wouldn't work. If there had been debate using *Robert's Rules* before the VISTA request had been submitted, I think they would have developed a better project. Nonetheless, I trudged on.

At Garrison, I had several opportunities to see how the entire school system operated. One evening the principal invited me to the PTA's Executive Committee meeting. All of the parents were upset because Garrison did not have new history textbooks. The next day I observed the principal calling the Baltimore City School's Book Depository. They told him they could not provide new books for the entire student body. He then asked for one set of books for one class to get the PTA off his back. PTA did not, as far as I could tell, follow *Robert's Rules*. There were no minutes. Everything was informal and transparency did not exist. One class of students got the books. The Executive Committee never knew the rest of the student body went wanting.

RONR devotes many pages to agendas. They can also apply to our own activities. As my year as a VISTA volunteer came to an end, I did not have a good agenda. I knew I would return to San Jose State but missed the deadline. VISTA was eager to keep volunteers so they accepted my application for another assignment. I was offered a job in the San Francisco Bay area and took on various assignments until I could return to school.

When I left VISTA I knew I wanted to play a role in eradicating poverty. With the war in Vietnam raging, anti-poverty funds dried up. To me, the Peace and Freedom Party (PFP) seemed to be the right vehicle for change.

I went home to Los Angeles and started knocking on doors to register people to vote. The State of California paid us to register voters. One afternoon I was answering phones in the PFP office when world famous record producer, conductor, arranger and composer, Quincy Jones, called. He wanted someone to come to his Mulholland Drive home to register him in the PFP. With my sister in tow, we went to his house. When I got back, I told our office manager we should send "heavyweights" to Jones' home to solicit money and support. The office manager said, "We don't want to treat people in our party differently" so he refused to do it. *Robert's Rules* would have been useful. Without bylaws and clearly defined leadership, I had nowhere to turn. Under a different scenario, a Board or Executive committee might have been empowered to make such a decision for the organization. I didn't want to make waves so I continued slogging away registering voters.

When I returned to San Jose State, I stayed with the party and was elected to the state steering committee. Without a firm grounding in *Robert's Rules*, I failed at my responsibility to keep others in the party informed. At a steering committee meeting in Los Angeles, I had a verbal dispute with fellow committee member Eldridge Cleaver, who received national notoriety for his best-selling book, *Soul on Ice.* Cleaver thought the Steering Committee should endorse a slate of candidates for President and Vice President. I felt we should have an open convention and asked him, "Don't you agree?" He said, "You see it your way. I see it mine." Unfortunately, he prevailed.

I attended PFP's first national convention in 1968 as an alternate delegate for Dick Gregory. Cleaver was nominated for President over Gregory. There wasn't much interest in following rules at the convention. Cleaver wasn't 35, therefore ineligible to run for president. After this, the Peace and Freedom Party drifted apart, and by the 1980's, Cleaver was publicly endorsing Ronald Reagan.

When I first became a student at San Jose State, the Academic Senate was a body made up of professors and administrators who met behind closed doors. Not even the press was allowed. When I returned, not only were meetings open but the organization had a new name: The *Student*, Faculty, Staff, Academic Senate. Nefarious power games were played. I was the victim of one of them. I was assigned to serve on the Calendar and Plant Committee. Week after week we met but in the end the administration presented their calendar and it was adopted.

Another duty was to weigh in on major building changes. We were given nothing to deal with but at the end of the year the administration announced a major construction project for the Drama Department. It was signed, sealed and delivered. We had no input but I stuck with it because I had the opportunity to ask hard-hitting questions to the newly appointed president, Dr. John Bunzel.

My life as an activist produced a pretty rich resume and a job as a Campus Activities Advisor at the University of Houston. There, from 1973 to 1978, I advised student organizations, including most prominently, the Program Council. All student organizations followed *Robert's Rules*, or so I thought. I later found out my boss "hated *Robert's Rules of Order*." I had my share of successes. A number of the committees that I advised received "Best of the Council" awards. One event stands out:

Congresswoman Barbara Jordan represented the area where the UH is located. The Forum Committee I advised asked her to come speak. She was prominent in the impeachment process involving President Richard Nixon and the Watergate scandal. The World Affairs Lounge held about 1,000 people. Attendance exceeded the fire code and the campus police had to secure the doors. At a University Center staff meeting the next day, I was raked over the coals for poor planning. Years later, a trusted mentor from San Jose State, Mary Hudziekiewicz, affirmed my belief that the primary job of an activities advisor was to make sure students stayed under control, and that students do nothing to disrupt the university.

In that role, I also had an opportunity to make a 20-minute presentation on *Robert's Rules*. The presentation received no support. Nevertheless, good things happened. The Campus Activities Department started a lifelong learning program called Sundry School. I played a key role and the program was a phenomenal success.

I left UH, and in 1979 started and co-directed for over 30 years Leisure Learning Unlimited, a lifelong learning program. For all those years and still today, I teach a class, "How to Have Great Meetings, The Basics of Robert's Rules of Order." I found out about the National Association of Parliamentarians, took their entrance exam, and became a member. The Pacifica Foundation is made up of five radio stations. One is in Houston and the others are in the largest cities in America. I helped re-write their bylaws in 2001 and have the distinction of being the longest serving parliamentarian in their recent history. Last year, I was paid to be a parliamentarian for a River Oaks Condominium Association (in the richest part of Houston.) Deloris Huerta, the co-founder (with Cesar Chavez) of the United Farm Workers Union, met me and bought a copy of my first book. I've been elected to be President of the Hermann Park Rotary Club, 2016-2017. And the best is yet to come.

Ted's Acknowledgments

In 2014, I self-published *Robert's Rules for Kids*. In that book, I acknowledged lots of people. Without them, this book would not exist. One person recognized previously, Juliet Stipeche, must be recognized again. At that time she was the President of the Houston Independent School Board and the trustee representing HISD's District VIII. She was familiar with what I brought to the table. When I asked her to introduce me to an elementary school principal who would test this project, she steered me in another direction.

That led to my meeting Dr. Bertie Simmons who returned to the ranks of the unretired in 2001 and became the Principal of Furr High School. She still holds that post in 2016. Before I met Dr. Simmons, I thought, for sure, she was a large African-American woman since I knew that she had turned a school with rampant gang problems into the school it is today. Imagine my surprise when I met this short, gray-haired Anglo. But her infectious laugh and positive attitude made me want to make this new project work.

I gave her my roadmap. Originally 50 students entered a competition to become part of a committee of 20 to write the bylaws that appear in this book. Off and on, about eight came early or stayed late to complete the task. Four, Trinity Payton, Madie Welch, Alice Ochoa, and Erika Canales, will be around next-year to see the election of the student government. Four others, Keyra Watson-Love and her twin sister Teyera, along with Pierre Davison and Abrilashay Swayzer are heading for college. The Watson-Love sisters deserve extra mention. They put in long hours just before Thanksgiving vacation in 2015 to finish an early important draft. The faculty of Furr High also deserves kudos. While I was pulling students out of class, they were supportive of the project. One teacher, Adrian Sendejas, was pushing for this even before I arrived on the scene. Without him, I don't know if the rest of the faculty would have been as supportive as they were. And Sharon Brown. She was the key person who gave me all the information about The Thinkery and Furr's Restorative Justice Program.

Because of Yates High School alum and parents, and future HISD School Board candidate, Gerry Monroe, this project got legs at Yates High School. Mr. Monroe, in one five-minute meeting, broke down whatever walls there were and gained me access to Principal Kenneth Davis. From there, I met teacher Joy Jackson and a similar project had wings at Yates. The students there, Isaiah Cooper, Kaylin

Jacobs, Rebecca Williams, Amber Felder, Gabrielle Braziel, TaiLyn Liggins, Joylissa Stafford, Madison Jenkins, Monet Simone Dixon, and Jalesha Bass, were enthusiastic about this project.

And then there's *Houston Chronicle* Business columnist (and author of *Tomlinson Hill*), Chris Tomlinson. I first met Chris Tomlinson at a ceremony that I attended with my spiritual brother, Jay Hamburger (who has fed the homeless on a weekly basis for over 20 years.) We were celebrating all-around good-guy Larry Payne at Interfaith Ministries for Greater Houston. Tomlinson showed interest in this book. It led to a full-page column (with picture) in the December 24, 2015, issue of the *Houston Chronicle*. What a present!

I would be remiss if I didn't thank again my partner, Sue Wittie, and my co-author Martha Haun. Without them, of course, none of these words would exist.

Peace,
Ted Weisgal

References

1.1 Cochran, Alice. *Roberta's Rules of Order: Sail Through Meetings for Stellar Results without the Gavel: A Guide for Nonprofits and Other Teams.* San Francisco, CA, Jossey-Bass, 2004, p. 12.

1.2 Robert, Henry M. (2011). *Robert's Rules of Order Newly Revised* (11th ed.). Philadelphia: Da Capo Press.

1.3 Putnam, Robert. *Bowling Alone: The Collapse and Revival of American Community,* New York, NY, Simon Schuster, 2000.

1.4 Pfeffer, Jeffrey. *Leadership BS: Fixing Workplaces and Careers One Truth at a Time.* [2015]

1.5 Place, Lucille. "The Next 20 Years." *Parliamentary Journal* January 1979, American Institute of Parliamentarians.

1.6 *Ibid.*

1.7 Weisgal, Ted. *Robert's Rules for Kids, a Guide to Teaching Children from Kindergarten to the 5th Grade: The Basics of Parliamentary Procedure.* Wise Wit Publishing. Houston, TX 2014.

1.8 Place, PJ, *Ibid.*

1.9 Sylvester, Nancy. *The Complete Idiot's Guide to Robert's Rules.* New York, NY: Alpha, 2004.

1.10 *American Institute of Parliamentarians Standard Code of Parliamentary Practice.* McGraw-Hill, New York 2012.

1.11 McElwain, Susan. "An Educational Rationale for the Inclusion of Parliamentary Procedure in the Elementary School Curriculum" *Parliamentary Journal,* 1980.

1.12 *Ibid.*

1.13 Robinson, Ken. *The Element: How Finding Your Passion Changes Everything.* New York, NY, Viking, 2009. Sir Kenneth Robinson is an English author, speaker, and international advisor on education in the arts to government, non-profits, education, and arts bodies. He was knighted in 2003 for services to education.

1.14 Goleman, Daniel. *Emotional Intelligence: Why It Matters More Than IQ.* Bantam Books: New York, NY. http://www.danielgoleman.info/topics/emotional-intelligence/Goleman is an author, psychologist and science journalist. A writer with *The New York Times,* he specializes in psychology and brain sciences.

1.15 Noelle-Neumann, Elisabeth. *The Spiral of Silence: Public Opinion–Our Social Skin.* Chicago: University of Chicago Press, 1984.

1.16 Costa, Arthur L. and Kallick, Bena. *Habits of Mind* Association for Supervision & Curriculum Development; 12/16/2008.

1.17 Sagan, Carl. National Public Radio (NPR) program *Science Friday.*

1.18 Friedman, Thomas. *Time to Take Teaching to a New Level*, published November 21, 2010. Quoted: Wagner, Tony. *The Global Achievement Gap.* 2008. New York, NY: Simon and Shuster. Tony Wagner, Ed. D., M.A.T. is Residence Expert the Innovation Lab at Harvard University. He was Co-Director at the Change Leadership Group at Harvard's Graduate School of Education. He worked as a high school teacher, an elementary school principal, university professor in teacher education, and was a founding executive director of Educators for Social Responsibility. He has written five books including *Creating Innovators: The Making of Young People Who will Change the World*. Wagner collaborated with filmmaker Robert Compton to create *"The Finland Phenomenon: Inside the World's Most Surprising School System."*

1.19 Navarrette, Jr., Ruben. Nationally syndicated columnist with *The Washington Post* Writer's Group, *Washington Post, February 8, 2014.* He is a member of the *USA Today* Board of Contributors, a regular commentator on NPR's "Tell Me More with Michelle Martin" and a weekly commentator for CNN.com, and author of *A Darker Shade of Crimson: Odyssey of a Harvard Chicano* (Bantam 1993).

1.20 Cushing, Luther S. (1847*). Manual of Parliamentary Procedure Practice: Rules of proceeding and debate in deliberative assemblies* (7th ed.). Boston: Taggard and Thompson.

1.21 Jefferson, Thomas. (1843). *A Manual of Parliamentary Practice*. Philadelphia: Hogan and Thompson.

1.22 Robert, Henry M. (1923). *Parliamentary Law*. New York: D. Appleton-Century Company.

1.23 American Institute of Parliamentarians. *Standard Code of Parliamentary Procedure.* McGraw-Hill, New York, 2012.

1.24 *RONR*, p. 202, ll 1-10.*1.14.*

Chapter 2

2.1 Possible books for review are:

Kaster, Pam. *Molly the Pony: A True Story*. Baton Rouge, LA. LSU Press, redistributed by Square Fish Books, a division of Macmillan Publishers, 2008.

Silverman, Erica and Lewin, Betsy. *Cowgirl Kate and Cocoa.* Boston, MA, HMH Books for Young Readers, 2005.

Smith, Ian & Julian, Sean. *Rooster's Alarm.* London, England, Hachette Children's Books, 2008.

2.2 http://www.readingrockets.org/audience/teachers

2.3 MacArthur, C. A., & Graham, S. (1987). Learning disabled students' composing under three methods of text production. *The Journal of Special Education*, 21(3), 22-42.

Stahl, S. A., Miller, P. D. (1989). Whole Language and Language Experience Approaches for Beginning Reading: A Quantitative Research Synthesis. *Review of Educational Research*, 59, 87-116.

Stauffer, Russell G. (1970). *The language experience approach to the teaching of reading.* New York: Harper & Row.

CHAPTER 3

3.1   Utah Layton Christian Academy; www.ulca.org

3.2   Texas /Assn. Student Councils; www.tasconline.org

3.3   Brooklyn Free School; brooklynfreeschoool.org

3.4   www.edpsycinteractive.org/topics/cognition/bloom.html

3.5   Fisher, B. Aubrey and Ellis, Donald. Small Group Decision Making: Communication and The Group Process McGraw-Hill, 1990. p. 34

3.6   Dewey, John. *How We Think.* 1910.

CHAPTER 4

4.1   Pearce, W. B. and Cronen, V. E. (1980) *Communication, Action and Meaning.* New York: Praeger.

4.2   Shimanoff. Susan. B. *Communication Rules: Theory and Research* (Beverly Hills, CA: Sage,1980) pp. 31-32.

4.3   *RONR* (11th ed.), XVIII "Bylaws", pp. 570-591.

APPENDICES

APPENDIX A: Bylaws of the Student Council of Furr High School

APPENDIX B: Bylaws of the Jack Yates High School Student Council

APPENDIX C: Event Guidelines

APPENDIX D: Business Meeting Sample Agenda

APPENDIX E: Sample Annual Calendar

APPENDIX F: Sports Column, Los Angeles Herald-Examiner, 1962

APPENDIX G: Chart of Motions

The two bylaws that follow (Appendices A & B) provide a good starting point for any student council. We recommend that a team of students and the principal modify and amend them to meet the needs of each school.

Appendix A:

Bylaws of the Student Council of Furr High School, Houston, TX

I. Name

The name of this organization shall be The Brahman Council of Furr High School.

II. Object

The object of the Brahman Council is to improve Furr High School through

a. increased student involvement in decision-making;
b. student applied tools in education, leadership, and order;
c. increased voice of the student body; and
d. increased sense of empowerment and confidence for students.

III. Membership

Section 1. There shall be one class of members: students in ninth, tenth, eleventh and twelfth grade.

Section 2. Students entering ninth grade shall not be eligible to vote for or serve on the Executive Board.

Section 3. Every student shall be a member of The Brahman Council as soon as they are fully enrolled in Furr High School. They lose their membership rights if they leave this school.

Section 4. Teachers, Administrators, Staff or Community Leaders

a. These individuals (maximum three) shall advise the Brahman Council.
b. They shall have no voting rights.
c. They shall be nominated by the Principal and approved by the Executive Committee and the Student Council.

Section 5. No fees shall be required for membership.

IV. **Officers and Duties**: Officers of the Student Council shall be the President, Vice-President, Secretary, Treasurer, Parliamentarian, and Historian. The officers shall perform the duties prescribed in these bylaws and the parliamentary authority *(RONR)*.

Section 1. The President shall:

a. Chair the Executive Board and the Student Council.
b. make applicable appointments. *(See Article VIII Section IV.)*
c. be the spokesperson for the Student Government (the Brahman Council).
d. attend at least two HISD Student Congress meetings keeping the Brahman Council updated on pertinent HISD matters.

Section 2. The Vice President shall:

a. monitor the activities of all committees;
b. provide regular reports to the Executive Board;
c. in the absence of the President, perform the duties of that office;
d. Chair such portions of Student Council meetings should the President choose to participate in debate during a section of the Student Council meetings; the Vice President may *(not should)* be selected to Chair.

Section 3. The Secretary shall:

a. be responsible for all of the current records including contact information of the Brahman Council.
b. take minutes in Executive Board and Student Council meetings, provide drafts to the applicable bodies and deliver final reports and minutes.
c. receive reports from all committees.
d. at the conclusion of his/her term *(if leaving office)*, provide said documents to his/her successor.

Section 4. The Treasurer shall:

a. share with the Principal or an adult designated by the Principal, the responsibility for receiving and depositing all funds from all Student Council entities.
b. co-sign *(with the Principal or their designate)* all Student Council checks or other payments.
c. maintain the books of the Student Council and regularly report to the Executive Board and the Student Council.

Section 6. The Parliamentarian shall:

a. serve at the discretion of the President;
b. become well-informed with the parliamentary authority;
c. advise the President when advice is requested;
d. with the approval of the President, may address one or more members of the Executive Board or Student Council;
e. not participate in debate as a member of the Executive Board or the Student Council and,
f. only vote when said vote is a secret ballot.

Section 7. The Historian shall:

a. serve as the keeper of the history of Furr High School;
b. maintain contact with the Secretary to insure accuracy and completeness of records;
c. serve as liaison for the media aspects of The Brahman Council (*including pictures, videos, and outreach etc.*)

V. Elections

Section 1. Nomination Procedure, Time of Elections.
During the last week of April or the first week of May, all ninth, tenth and eleventh grade students shall have the right to nominate themselves or someone else for any or all elective offices, but shall do so privately, in writing.

a. Only the School Secretary and Principal shall know who has been nominated. *[If a parent or guardian does not want their son/daughter to be nominated for any office, they may have on record a statement to this effect.]*
b. On the day of the election, each candidate willing to accept the nomination shall come to the Conference Room in the Main Office where they will be given 15 minutes to write a speech, (maximum one 8 1/2" x 11" statement) in support of their candidacy for each office to which they have been nominated. This statement (or statements) may include answers to questions about the office to which they are running that have been reviewed by the Principal. Completed statements will be broadcast, using the school's public address system.
c. Readers shall be selected by the Principal for their oral reading skills.
d. Each candidate will be identified only by number.
e. Students will vote on this basis. There will be no advance campaigning.

f. If a person is elected to more than one office, they shall have the choice of which office they wish to assume or take the highest office based on the ranked list (see Article IV, Section 1).
g. The runner-up for the office which the winner does not select will be declared the winner of that office.

Section 2. Ballot Election, Term of Office, Removal from Office.
Elections shall be determined by secret ballot that shall take place in each classroom and supervised by the ranking teacher *(if there is more than one teacher in that class)*. The ballots will be counted publicly in each classroom and the vote count will be delivered by a team of at least two members to the School Secretary as soon as it is completed.

a. As a backup, the teacher shall also provide these results by the end of the school day. If there are any irregularities or discrepancies, a recount on the next school day shall take place. A revote shall be supervised by the Principal or their designate.
b. An unofficial result shall be announced by eighth period on the day of the election;
c. an official result shall be announced by the end of the subsequent week. Any irregularities shall be examined by the Nominations and Elections Committee and reported to the Brahman Council who shall hold a hearing and make a ruling which shall include the possibility of expulsion of a candidate. The Principal may hear appeals and make a final decision.

Section 3. Failure to Achieve a Majority. If, in the first round of voting, no candidate receives a majority vote and the two top candidates are not able to determine between themselves the winner, there shall be a runoff election the next school day between these two individuals.

a. In the runoff, the highest candidates shall be declared the winner. Note: All candidates for the contested office shall report to the main office while voting is taking place. Prior to voting, students should hear a new speech from these two finalists using the same method described earlier *(V, Section 1, b-e.)*

Section 4. Failure to Perform Duties. For either nonfeasance or malfeasance, officers may be removed from office at the pleasure of the membership following the rules provided in Chapter XX of RONR.

Section 5. Office-Holding Limitations.

a. No member shall hold more than one office at a time except that officers may also serve as Ambassadors should there be a need.

VI. Meetings

Section 1. Regular meetings of the Student Council shall be held one time per month.

Section 2. Advocacy shall meet once a week during homeroom.

Section 3. Special Meetings. Special meetings of The Brahman Council to hear complaints about members of the organization that could lead to and include removal from office may, with approval of the Principal, be called by the President, a majority of the Executive Board, or a written request of ten students of the school. The purpose of the meeting shall be stated in the call, which shall be sent to all members at least seven days before the meeting.

Section 4. Order of Business. For the Advocacy Committee, The Brahman Council, and Executive Board meetings. Reading and Approval of Minutes

  a. Reading and Approval of Minutes means that the Secretary and the Historian should have the accurate information of each meeting. Minutes shall include what was discussed throughout the meeting (*including questions, answers, events, etc.*)*

  *This is a departure from what RONR recommends. Unless it is noted that what the Secretary has written is just opinion, it can result in many disputes.

  b. Reports of Officers, Boards, and Standing Committees
  c. Reports of Special Committees
  d. Unfinished Business
  e. New Business

Section 5. Quorum. Fifty per cent of the members of The Brahman Council shall constitute a quorum for both Regular and Special Meetings. In Advocacy meetings, the persons present shall constitute a quorum.

VII. Executive Board and Duties

Section 1. Board Composition. The officers of this organization shall constitute the Executive Board.

Section 2. Board's Duties. The Executive Board, through their Secretary, shall receive reports from the Chairs and committees. They shall also prepare the outline of an agenda for Regular and Special Meetings of the Student Council. Items under the heading New Business may be added during the Brahman Council meeting.

Section 3. Board Meetings. Executive Board meetings shall be scheduled twice per month and also upon the call of fifty percent of the Executive Board members. Expulsion by missing three meetings in a row with the exception of certified health reasons or for an absence excused by the Principal. Ten students may call for a special meeting.

VIII. **Committees and Subcommittees**

   Section 1. Nominations and Elections Committee.

   a. Shall consist of five graduating seniors, who shall work with three non-voting adult officials appointed by the Principal to oversee the nominations and election process;
   b. Elected students will serve the following school year. Students who are going to repeat the 12th grade may not serve on this committee.

   Section 2: Advocacy Committee

   a. Each Advocacy class shall constitute a committee. The President of the Brahman Council shall appoint a temporary Chair. A Chair should be elected by that class during the second week of school utilizing the approach described in RONR as "filling blanks."
   b. It shall be the prerogative of the applicable period's teacher in consultation with his/her class to determine how much time may be devoted to speeches and a vote.

   Section 3: Chairs. Chairs are responsible for receiving motions *(New Business)* from their Advocacy Committee and deliver them to the Executive Board who shall place them on the agenda for the next Student Council meeting. Before the Student Council votes on any motion, Chair must be given the opportunity to poll their Advocacy Committee. When this item appears on the agenda a second time it will be treated as Unfinished Business.

   Section 4. Fall Election. Each Chair will represent their Advocacy Committee on the Student Council for a semester. During the twelfth week of the fall semester, each Advocacy Committee will determine if they wish to re-elect their Chair, should that person choose to run.

   Section 5. Special Committees. The President, the Executive Board, or the Student Council by majority vote, may establish Special Committees that shall report to the Executive Board and Student Council. The President shall be an ex officio (non-voting) member of Special Committees. Each Advocacy Committee (mentioned in Section 2, above) shall have the prerogative of establishing their own sub-committees that report to their Advocacy Committee and then to their Chair who will deliver written reports to the

Executive Board and to the Student Council. The Chair(s) of sub-committees shall be determined by members of subcommittees. Sub-committees may alternate/rotate the duties of their Chairs.

IX. Parliamentary Authority

The rules contained in the current edition of *Robert's Rules of Order Newly Revised* shall govern the Society in all cases to which they are applicable and in which they are not inconsistent with Federal law, state of Texas law, Houston Independent School District law, these bylaws, and any Special Rules the Student Council may adopt.

X. Amendment of Bylaws

These bylaws may be amended at any regular meeting of the Student Council by a 2/3 vote, provided that (1) the amendment has been submitted in writing at the previous meeting; (2) opportunity has been provided for review by all advocacy committees; and, (3) proposal has been approved by the Principal.

Appendix B:

Bylaws of the Jack Yates High School Student Government

Article I. Name.

The name of this organization shall be the Jack Yates High School Student Government.

Article II. Purpose.

The purposes of the Jack Yates Student Council shall be to:

1. Practice group politics and economics so that actions taken can be mirrored by the community.
2. Rebuild the democratic structure of the school as a model to the community.
3. Create a student government that reflects democratic process and gives voice to all students at Jack Yates High School.
4. Establish a process through which recommendations adopted by the students, working through their respective class Vice Presidents and the Executive Committee, may petition the Principal for final approval.

Article III. Membership

Section 1. There shall be one class of voting membership: students in grades 9, 10, 11 and 12. However, students entering 9th grade shall not be eligible to vote for or serve on the Executive Committee until they have been elected to serve as an Ambassador by their Advocacy class. These Ambassadors shall have the right to run for the position of 9th grade Vice President. That election shall occur as soon as possible at the beginning of the school year and shall mirror the other school-wide elections.

Section 2. Students will become members of *the Jack Yates Student Government* as soon as they are fully enrolled in Jack Yates High School. They will lose their membership rights if they leave this school.

Section 3. Teachers, Administrators, Staff or Community Leaders.

A. These individuals numbering a maximum of 5 will be limited to advise the organization.
B. They will have no voting rights.
C. They will be appointed by the Principal.

Article IV. Officers

Section 1. Officers.

a. The officers of the Student Council (the Executive Committee) shall be the President, Four Vice-Presidents, the Secretary, Treasurer, Historian and Parliamentarian.
b. The officers shall perform the duties prescribed by these bylaws and the parliamentary authority, *Robert's Rules of Order Newly Revised, 11th ed.*

Section 2. Duties of the President.

a. The President shall Chair the Executive Committee and the Student Council.
b. The President of the Student Government may make applicable appointments.
c. This student shall be the spokesperson for the Student Government.

Section 3. Duties of the Vice Presidents

a. There shall be four Vice Presidents, one for each grade.
b. The 12th grade Vice President will be the first in line to succeed the President, should the President be unable to fulfill his/her duties. The line of succession after that will be the 11th, 10th, and 9th grade Vice Presidents.
c. Each Vice President shall monitor the activities of the committees of his/her class and provide reports to the Executive Committee.
d. Vice Presidents shall meet with their Ambassadors as a group prior to each Executive Committee Meeting at a time and place determined by the Vice President. Each Vice President shall select a faculty member to serve as their advisor.
e. In the absence of the President, the Vice President shall perform the President's duties.
f. Should the President wish to participate in debate during a section of the Student Council meetings, the Sr. Class Vice President shall Chair.
g. Vice Presidents shall divide up supervisory duties for other non-class related committees.

Section 4. Duties of the Secretary.

a. The Secretary shall be responsible for all the records including contact information of the Student Government.
b. This person shall take minutes in Executive Committee and Student Council meetings, provide drafts to the applicable bodies and deliver final reports and minutes.
c. The Secretary shall receive reports from all committees. At the conclusion of his/her term *(if leaving office)* he/she shall provide said documents to his/her successor.

Section 5. Duties of the Treasurer.

a. The Treasurer shall share with the Principal, or an adult designated by the Principal, the responsibility for receiving and depositing all funds from all Student Council entities.
b. The Treasurer shall co-sign *(with the Principal or their designate)* all Student Government checks or other payments.
c. The Treasurer shall maintain the books of the Student Government and report regularly to the Executive Committee and the Student Council.

Section 6. Duties of the Historian.

a. The Historian shall be responsible for maintaining all records of the Jack Yates Student Government including agendas, minutes, reports, newspaper articles and other memorabilia.
b. The Historian shall pass this information on from one administration to the next.

Section 7. Duties of the Parliamentarian.

a. The Parliamentarian shall be selected by and serve at the discretion of the President.
b. The Parliamentarian shall advise the President when advice is requested.
c. Upon the approval of the President, the Parliamentarian may address one or more members of the Executive Committee or Student Council.
d. The Parliamentarian may not participate in debate as a member of the Executive Committee or the Student Council.
e. The Parliamentarian may only vote when said vote is a secret ballot.

Article V. Student Council

Section 1. Composition. The Student Council shall be comprised of one delegate Ambassador selected from each homeroom. Ambassadors may self-nominate, shall be elected by majority vote, and shall represent the interests of their constituency.

Section 2. Term of Office. Ambassadors shall (1) be elected in the spring for a term of one academic year starting with the fall term and serving until May; or, until a successor is elected. An ambassador may serve more than one term.

Section 3. Removal from Office. An Ambassador may be removed from office for (1) a failing grade; (2) violation of HISD/Yates H.S. policies; or, by direction of the principal. The principal shall determine whether the removal is permanent or temporary.

Section 4. Time of Elections. The advisory board in consultation with the principal shall set the exact time of elections, usually late in the spring semester.

Article VI. Elections

Section 1. Nomination Procedure, Time of Elections.

a. In the spring, during the week third week of April, any ninth, tenth or eleventh grade student may be nominated to be one or more of the aforementioned officers except Parliamentarian.
b. Students may self-nominate or nominate any other member of the student body. The person being nominated has the right to decline.
c. Nominations shall be given to the designate of the Principal for recording purposes and then to the Nominations and Elections Committee.
d. Members of the Nominations and Elections Committee must show no favoritism toward any candidate. Failure to remain impartial, as determined by a majority of the Nominations and Elections Committee, shall result in removal from the Nominations and Elections Committee.
e. All nominations shall be posted in a prominent public area upon receipt of the nomination. Candidates will be given the opportunity to place five campaign posters no larger than 11" by 17" on the walls of the campus and in the cafeteria. Locations will be determined on a first come, first served basis.
f. Candidates will be given the opportunity to give speeches not exceeding 45 seconds over the school public address system. The scheduling of time will be determined by the Principal.
g. Campaigning before and after school as well as between classes is also permitted.
h. Candidates who are late for class due to campaigning will lose this privilege.

Section 2. Ballot Election, Term of Office, Removal from Office.

a. Elections shall be determined by secret electronic ballot.
b. Any irregularities or discrepancies shall be addressed by the Nominations and Elections Committee.
c. If an election is ruled invalid by this committee, a revote shall be supervised by the Principal or their designate.
d. An unofficial result shall be announced by the last period on the day of the election; an official result shall be announced by the end of the subsequent week.
e. Any irregularities shall be examined by the Nominations and Elections
f. Committee and reported to the Student Council (or for the first election, by the Principal) who shall hold a hearing and make a ruling which shall include the possibility of expulsion of a candidate from the race.
g. The Principal may hear appeals before making a final decision.

Section 3. Failure to Achieve a Majority.

a. The candidate who receives the greatest number of votes (possibly a plurality) shall be declared the winner.

Section 4. Failure to Perform.

a. For either nonfeasance or malfeasance, officers may be removed from office at the pleasure of the membership following the rules provided in Chapter XX of RONR. Should someone be removed, they will be replaced by someone selected by the Student Council except for the President who will be succeeded by the 12th Grade Vice President.

Section 5. Office-Holding Limitations. No member shall hold more than one office at a time including that of an Ambassador.

Article VII. Meetings

Section 1. Regular meetings of the **Student Council** shall be held nine times per school year, once every month, and shall be held during the Advocacy period.

Section 2. Meetings of the **Executive Committee** shall be held every Wednesday after school between 3:15 and 4:15 pm. **Special Meetings** of the Executive Committee shall also be held upon the call of 25% the Executive Committee.

Section 3. Special Meetings. Special meetings of the Student Council to hear complaints about members of the organization that could lead to and include removal from office may, with approval of the Principal, be called by the President, a majority of the Executive Committee, or a written request of 10% of students of the school. The purpose of the meeting shall be stated in the call, which shall be sent to all members at least three full school days before the meeting.

Section 4. Order of Business

For all meetings, the standard order of business shall be:

   I. Reading and Approval of Minutes
   II. Reports of Officers, Boards, and/or Standing Committees
   III. Reports of Special Committees
   IV. Unfinished Business
   V. New Business

This may be changed by a 2/3 vote without previous notice.

Section 5. Quorum. 10% of the members of the Student Council shall constitute a quorum for both Regular and Special Meetings. In Advocacy meetings, the students present shall constitute a quorum.

**Article VIII. Executive Committee and Duties;
Student Council and Duties**

Section 1. Composition: Executive Committee. The officers of this organization shall constitute the Executive Committee.

Section 2. Duties. The Executive Committee, through their Secretary, shall receive reports from the class Vice Presidents and committees. They shall also prepare the outline of an agenda for Regular and Special Meetings of the Student Council. Items under the heading New Business may be added during the Student Council meeting.

Section 3. Composition: Student Council. The officers of this organization and the Ambassadors shall constitute the Student Council.

Section 4. Duties. The Student Council shall be the body that passes motions and makes recommendations to the Principal.

Article IX. Committees and Subcommittees

Section 1. Nominations and Elections Committee. The Nominations and Elections Committee, limited to graduating seniors, shall work with non-voting adult officials appointed by the Principal to oversee the nomination and election process that will elect students for the following school year. Students who are going to repeat the 12th grade may not serve on this committee.

Section 2: Classroom Committees. Each Advocacy class shall constitute a committee. The President of the Student Council shall appoint a temporary Chair/Ambassador. A Chair/Ambassador should be elected by said class during the 2nd week of school (fall semester) using the approach described in RONR as "filling blanks." It shall be the prerogative of the applicable period's teacher in consultation with his/her class to determine how much time may be devoted to speeches and voting.

Section 3: Chairs/Ambassadors. Chairs/Ambassadors are responsible for receiving motions *(New Business)* from their class/committee and delivering them to their class Vice President who shall bring them to the Executive Committee. Before the Student Council votes on any motion, Ambassadors must be given the opportunity to poll their Advocacy class. When this item appears on the agenda a second time, it will be treated as Unfinished Business.

Section 4. Representation. Each Ambassador will represent their Advocacy class on the Student Council for a semester or the entire school year. During the final month of the fall semester, each Advocacy class will determine if they wish to re-elect their Ambassador, should that person choose to run.

Section 5. Special Committees. The President, the Executive Committee, or the Student Council by majority vote may establish Special Committees that shall report to the Executive Committee and Student Council. The President shall be an ex officio (non-voting) member of Special Committees.

Section 6. Subcommittees. Each Advocacy class (mentioned in Section 2, above) shall have the prerogative of establishing their own sub-committees that (a) report to their Advocacy class and then (b) to their Ambassador who will deliver written reports to the Executive Committee and then, (c) spoken reports to the Student Council. The Chair(s) of sub-committee(s) shall be determined by members of sub-committees. Sub-committees may alternate/rotate the duties of their Chairs.

Article X. Advisory Board

Section 1. Membership. A maximum of five teachers, administrators, staff or community leaders shall be appointed by the principal to serve as advisors to the Student Council.

Section 2. Authority. The members of the Advisory Board shall have no vote on the Executive Committee but shall make their recommendations to the Principal, the Executive Committee, and the Student Council.

Article XI: Parliamentary Authority

Section 1. The rules contained in the current edition of *Robert's Rules of Order Newly Revised* shall govern the Society in all cases to which they are applicable and in which they are not inconsistent with laws of the United States, the State of Texas, the Houston Independent School District, as well as these bylaws and any Special Rules the Student Council may adopt.

Article XII. Amendment of Bylaws

These bylaws may be amended at any regular meeting of the Student Council by a 2/3 vote, provided that the amendment has been submitted in writing at the previous meeting, had the opportunity to be reviewed by all classroom committees, and been approved by the Principal.

NOTE: When there is a vote requiring 2/3, that is usually a counted vote; voice votes are seldom appropriate. In the case where there is a majority vote, only when there is doubt by either the President, an Ambassador, or the members, should there be a counted vote. ***Abstentions are meaningless and therefore should be ignored (an exception being to indicate that a quorum was present).***

Adopted (this date) _____, 2016, by the representatives of Jack Yates High School, Houston, TX.

_____
Student Representative, Jack Yates High School

_____
Advisory Board Member

_____
Principal, Jack Yates High School

Appendix C:
EVENT GUIDELINES
Parliamentary Procedure Guidelines (February 2011)

PARLIAMENTARY PROCEDURE

Purpose: To develop leadership skills by using parliamentary procedure to conduct a simulated business meeting. This event is based on team competition; therefore, members learn the importance of cooperation and working together through competitive performance.

Description This event will involve two rounds of competition. Round One will consist of a written test of Event: to evaluate the team's understanding of parliamentary procedure. The top scoring teams will advance to Round Two and will be given a secret problem with motions to perform during the meeting. The team has ten (10) minutes preparation time prior to the ten (10) minute demonstration of the meeting. All team members must be involved in the meeting.

Dress Code: Competitors shall wear the HOSA uniform or proper business attire. Bonus points will be awarded for proper dress in both rounds. All team members must be properly dressed to receive bonus points.

Rules and Procedures:
1. Competitors in this event must be active members of HOSA in good standing in the category in which they are registered to compete (Secondary or Postsecondary/ Collegiate).
2. Teams shall be composed of five (5) to eight (8) members with identified offices or representative thereof (i.e., president, treasurer, committee Chairman, member, *etc.*)
3. Each team will be evaluated in Round One by a one hundred (100) item multiple choice written test. Competitors will be given 1 ½ hours to complete the test given during the event orientation session.

No proxies are allowed for this event.
Team scores will be averaged to determine who will qualify for Round Two.
Test Plan: From the National Association of Parliamentarians 100%
- Basic Rules, Procedures and Handling of a Motion
- Basic Classifications & Descriptions
- Meeting, Session, Recess & Adjournment
- Main Motion
- Subsidiary Motions
- Privileged Motions
- Incidental Motions
- Motions That Bring a Question Again Before the Assembly

- Quorum and Order of Business
- Debate & Voting
- Officers & Officer Reports

4. A maximum of twenty (20) Secondary and ten (10) Postsecondary/Collegiate teams will advance to Round Two. Team numbers and appointment times are preassigned on a random selection basis.
5. Each team prepares, in advance, minutes of a previous local chapter meeting with a treasurer's report and committee report(s) that are brought to the presentation room and used according to parliamentary law.
6. In the preparation room, each member of the team will be given a copy of the secret problem and will have ten (10) minutes to plan their meeting. Team members are permitted to write on their copy of the secret problem.

EVENT GUIDELINES
Parliamentary Procedure Guidelines (February 2011)
7. Teams will then have ten (10) minutes to present their meeting for the judges. All members of the team will be allowed to have a copy of the secret problem during the competition. Minutes MAY be written on the secretary's copy.
8. Parliamentary references (including but not limited to *Robert's Rules of Order, Newly Revised)* may be used by the team during this preparation period but not during the presentation.
9. The secret problem will include at least six (6) different motions from at least three (3) of the five (5) classes of motions: main, subsidiary, privileged, incidental and motions that bring a question before the assembly.
10. Only the following items may be taken into the presentation room: a copy of the minutes of the preceding meeting, the treasurer's report, committee report(s), copies of the secret problem for each team member, blank paper and pen to record the minutes of the meeting, and pencil for president to take notes during the meeting.
11. The presentation is to consist of procedures that should be used in a complete regular business meeting (i.e., call to order through adjournment). The secret problem contains motions that must be included in the presentation in the appropriate order of business and in the order presented on the written secret problem. Other topics may also be taken up during the presentation.
12. The secret problem for this event is confidential information. Professional ethics demand that competitors DO NOT discuss or reveal the secret topic until after the event has concluded. Competitors who violate this ethical standard will be disqualified.
13. The team is seated so that the judges have a full view of the participants.
14. Each team is allowed ten (10) minutes beginning with the sound of gavel at opening and ending with the sound of the gavel at closing. The timekeeper stands at the end of the 8 minutes and remains standing to indicate that 2 minutes remain. At the end of 10 minutes, the timekeeper will stop the team.

The secretary will be given two (2) minutes to complete an outline of the minutes of the meeting to be given to the judges. The minutes are rated for accuracy to include motion, names, and actions in an outline form and are not to be a rewritten narrative.

15. *Robert's Rules of Order Newly Revised* (Latest Edition), by General Henry M. Robert, Scott Foresman and Company: Glenview, IL, shall be the official parliamentary authority reference for this event. Other references included are:
    • *Study Questions for NAP Membership Exam, 10th Edition,* National Association of Parliamentarians.
16. Should a tie occur, the highest team average from the written test will be used to break the tie.

EVENT GUIDELINES
Parliamentary Procedure Guidelines (February 2011)

Appendix D:
Business Meeting: Sample Agenda

BUSINESS MEETING #1

AGENDA

THURSDAY, APRIL 28, 2020 9:00 a.m. – BALLROOM A

Call to Order/Welcoming Remarks .... Marjorie Saulson

Opening Ceremony

    Posting of the Colors

    Canadian and United States National Anthems

    (Lyrics on next page)

WELCOME

Credentials Committee Report .... Juliana Pleines

Approval of Agenda .... Marjorie Saulson

Introductions: Directors, Parliamentarian, Past Presidents,

    Past Board Members .... Marjorie Saulson

Introductions: Delegations .... Ann Philbin

Approval of Minutes of 2019 Conference .... Marjorie Saulson

    Minutes approval committee:
    1. Wendy Kelman – Los Angeles
    2. Michael Minor – Kansas City
    3. Ann Philbin - Boston

Appointment of 2020 Reading Committee .... Marjorie Saulson

Treasurer's Financial Report .... Judith Konen

NEW BUSINESS
Presentation of 2021 Conference Invitation .... Juliana Pleines

Bylaws, Standing Rules & Policy Amendments .... Heather Moore

Review of Nomination Procedure and Voting Kit .... Heather Moore

ELECTIONS
Conference Announcements .... Marjorie Saulson, Helen Shaffer

ADJOURNMENT

APPENDIX E:

Sample Annual Calendar for Implementation of a Student Government

Please note: This calendar is designed for grades K-5; 6-8 and 9-12 with school beginning in August and ending for summer vacation by the end of May. Modify it for your own needs.

JULY: Begin planning an in-service where all teachers are apprised of the calendar for the year and the tasks that will fall to them. Begin preparing any materials that will be required.

AUGUST: Hold an in-service: **For elementary school teachers**, determine if the model that includes 4th graders meeting with a kindergartener and a 5th grader meeting with a group of 1st graders is going to be in force or if all activities are going to take place in class, or both. Do role-playing exercises that illustrate what will take place and discuss the merits of each in a committee of the whole. At **middle and high school levels**, have a number of committee meetings where teachers will role-play students holding committee meetings. Then take the committee reports to a mock student council meeting where teachers will play the role of students. See *Robert's Rules* in action. As part of the in-service, explore ways democratic decision making can complement existing curriculum. Example: For the spring choral performance, let the students decide if there will be soloists or only ensemble pieces.

EARLY SEPTEMBER: Hold campus-wide elections following the bylaws that the students have adopted. Have assemblies or the like where candidates' positions are shared with the voters. Announce the results of the campus-wide elections and have homeroom meetings where the election of ambassadors takes place. **MID-SEPTEMBER**: Start having executive committee and homeroom committee meetings. **LATE SEPTEMBER**: Have Student Council meetings and as a first order of business, develop a campus-wide calendar for the next seven months.

OCTOBER, NOVEMBER, DECEMBER, JANUARY, FEBRUARY, MARCH, APRIL: Have committee, executive committee and Student Council meetings following the schedule adopted late September by Student Council and approved by the principal. As necessary, have faculty meetings where problems and successes with the student government are addressed.

DECEMBER: If students decide that they are going to change ambassadors for the spring semester, this is when in-class elections should take place.

MAY: Announce that it is time for students to declare their candidacy for the fall elections. All classes and students will have the summer to develop platforms and to prepare materials for the fall. Only incoming classes will miss out on this opportunity unless information is provided to the schools in the feeder pattern. Kindergarten is included in materials provided to parents of incoming students.

Appendix F:
Sports Column, Los Angeles Herald-Examiner, 1962

Ten years after this column, written by co-author Ted Weisgal, was published, the United States Federal Government passed Title IX. Title IX is a law that requires public schools that receive federal funds to provide opportunities for girls to participate in extracurricular activities, including sports, equal to that which boys receive. Change in education can be slow. We hope adding Robert's Rules to the curriculum is faster.

THE PREP FRONT
Don't Laugh Fellows!
By Ted Weisgal
SSA Editor–Poly

Years ago, the concept of girls competing in athletics on the same level as boys would have been ridiculed no end. But today this is common practice in some areas of Southern California. Not so in Los Angeles. Girls in Orange, Riverside and San Diego Counties are given nearly the same competitive athletic outlet as boys and there is no evidence to indicate they become muscle-bound Amazons.

Educators in our town, however, believe that interscholastic sports for girls is not good "because of their temperament," according to Guy Wrinkle, athletic supervisor for the L.A. City Schools.

"Boys love to fight and do battle; girls would cry after losing," Wrinkle said.

Wrinkle's views were contradicted, however, by R. Bruce Munro, vice principal at San Jacinto High School, in whose area girl's tennis is on an interscholastic level.

Just as Good Sports

"The girls still aren't getting enough competition," said Munro. "They're just as good sports as the boys.

We never had any problem with temperament but how can a girl become a good sport if she doesn't learn to go through actual competition?"

Munro opined that all the good points of boys' athletics—teamwork, character building, etc.—would apply to girls' athletics.

Ken Fagans, CIF Southern Section athletic commissioner, agreed with Munro in pointing out that girls participated along with the boys in major prep tennis tournaments such as the Dudley Cup in Santa Monica and the yearly Ojai netfest.

A stringent viewpoint is expressed by Miss Evangeline Reynolds, girl's athletic supervisor for the L.A. schools, who flatly states, "the policy of the Board of

Education is against girls competing interscholastically. It is not in accord with our philosophy on the girl's physical education program."

A more tempered viewpoint comes from Miss Miriam Paine, assistant supervisor of physical education in the San Diego City Schools, who says competitive athletics is a healthful outlet for girls.

Although there are no interscholastic leagues as such for San Diego girls, they are offered the chance to compete in basketball, softball, volleyball, track and gymnastics throughout the year.

Olympic Team Member from Marshall

Another female who is deeply involved in the situation is Carolyn House, 1960 Olympic Games swimming team member who speaks from her vantage point as a student at Marshall High.

"Most girls can take it just like boys," Carolyn said in defending her sex. She also advocated the formation of leagues in swimming, tennis, golf, basketball, track and gymnastics.

A program which offers Orange County girls competition in field hockey, volleyball, swimming softball, basketball and badminton was outlined by Frank O. Hopkins, superintendent of the Brea Olinda High School District.

Although Hopkins points out that these occasions are more a social than sporting event, he says the individual sports—tennis golf, swimming, etc.—are "excellent for girls."

All reports would indicate that our country cousin" counties have a big lead in recognizing that women's suffrage includes the right to enjoy stimulating athletics competition.

Who says Los Angeles is the sports capital of the world?

Appendix G:
CHART OF MOTIONS

CHART I: Ranking Motions with Standard Characteristics

	MOTION	May interrupt when another has the floor	Requires a second	Debatable	Amendable	Vote Required for Adoption	Can it be reconsidered
Privileged Motions	Fix Time to Which to Adjourn	No	Yes	No	Yes	Majority	Yes
	Adjourn	No	Yes	No	No	Majority	No
	Recess (include length of time)	No	Yes	No	Yes	Majority	No
	Raise a Question of Privilege	Yes	No	No	No	None Chair handles	No
	Call for Orders of the Day (agenda)	Yes	No	No	No	Chair handles	No
Subsidiary Motions	Lay on the Table/Postpone Temporarily	No	Yes	No	No	Majority	Negative Only
	Previous Question/Move to Close Debate	No	Yes	No	No	Two-thirds	Yes
	Limit or Extend Limits of Debate	No	Yes	No	Yes	Two-thirds	Yes
	Postpone to Certain Time	No	Yes	Yes	Yes	Majority	Yes
	Commit or Refer to a Committee	No	Yes	Yes	Yes	Majority	Yes
	Amend	No	Yes	Yes***	Yes	Majority	Yes
	Postpone Indefinitely	No	Yes	Yes	No	Majority	Yes*
	Main Motion	No	Yes**	Yes	Yes	Majority	Yes

Note: Motions on this chart are listed in order of "rank," beginning with Main Motion, which is lowest. When a motion is amendable but not debatable, any amendments to such motion are undebatable. Call for the Orders of the Day and Question of Privilege require no vote—only action by the Chair.
* Affirmative vote only.
** A motion made by a committee of two or more members does not require a second.
***If applied to a debatable motion.

CHART II: Common Incidental Motions with Standard Characteristics

INCIDENTAL MOTIONS (not ranked)	In order when another has the floor	Requires a second	Debatable	Amendable	Vote Required for Adoption	Can be reconsidered
Point of Order	Yes	No	No	No	None	No
Appeal	Yes	Yes	Yes	No	Majority[1]	Yes
Suspend the Rules	No	Yes	No	No	Two-thirds	No
Objection to Consideration	Yes	No	No	No	2/3 in neg.	Neg. vote only
Division of a Question	No	Yes	No	Yes	Majority	No
Consideration by Paragraph	No	Yes	No	Yes	Majority	No
Division of the Assembly	Yes	No	No	No	None[2]	No
Motions relating to voting and nominations	No	Yes	No	Yes	Majority[3]	Yes[4]
Requests and Inquiries	Yes	No	No[5]	No[5]	Majority[6]	No
Request for a Privilege	Yes	No	No	No	Majority	No

1. Majority or tie vote sustains the decision of the Chair
2. On the demand of a single member, the Chair must take a rising vote
3. Except motion to close polls or affirmative vote on motion to reopen polls
4/5. Except Request to be Excused from a duty
6. Except Parliamentary Inquiry and Request for Information (formerly and still accepted Point of Information), which require no vote

CHART III: Restoratory Motions (Bring Back) with Standard Characteristics

Restoratory (or Bring Back Motions)	In order when another has the floor	Requires a second	Debatable	Amendable	Vote Required for Adoption	Can be reconsidered
Take from the Table	No	Yes	No	No	Majority	No
Reconsider (at same meeting)	No[(1)]	Yes	Yes[(2)]	No	Majority	No
Rescind (at a subsequent meeting)	No	Yes	Yes	Yes	Two-thirds[(3)]	Negative vote only
Amend Something Previously Adopted	No	Yes	Yes	Yes	Two-thirds[(3)]	Negative vote only
Discharge a Committee	No	Yes	Yes	Yes	Two-thirds[(4)]	Negative vote only

5. The making of the motion is in order when another has the floor, but before the speaker begins.
6. Is debatable ONLY if the motion to be reconsidered is debatable
7. Or majority if previous notice is given, or majority of the entire membership.
8. Or majority if previous notice is given.

For More Information

Robert's Rules for Kids Website
www.RobertsRulesforKids.com

Author's Facebook Page
https://www.facebook.com/ted.weisgal
https://www.facebook.com/martha.haun

Author's LinkedIn Page
http://www.linkedin.com/pub/martha-haun/

Contact the Authors for workshops or to speak to your school or group:
Martha Haun: mhaun@uh.edu
Ted Weisgal: tedweisgal@gmail.com

Much of society is still dysfunctional and no longer works. Special interest groups often use bullying tactics to make others submit to their agenda. This leaves many people without a voice. To have an effective society, we need effective organizations. To have equality for all, we need to hear everyone's voice, not just those who scream the loudest, have the most money, or control the information flow.

Democracy is for everyone. Learn the fundamental principles of order from a guide designed for teachers who work with students from kindergarten through the 12th grade but is beneficial for "kids of all ages."

Rules of Order used to be taught to many school-aged children. It provided a structure for communication and problem solving where elite members of the student body could be heard. Yet even elite students are unfamiliar with Robert's Rules of Order. Robert's currently does not exist in the curriculum.

Imagine a better world where everyone's concerns were listened to and valued. What if there was a system that could fix it? The easy part is done. Here's our curriculum. We hope you find this book as useful as we find the subject fascinating. Go forth and do good work!

Martha Womack Haun, Ph.D., PRP
Ted Weisgal

Made in the USA
Coppell, TX
14 November 2020